The Hors d' Oeuvre Tray

VOLUME I

Compiled by:

Mrs. Ray Bennett
Mrs. Brad Burnette
Mrs. Jeff Moritz
Mrs. Charlie Powers
Mrs. Fred Ware

Cover photo: Jimmy Jamison

Edited by: Mrs. Richard Anderson

Designed by: Richard Anderson

International Standard Book Number 0-918544-03-3

table of contents

Printed in the United States of America by

WIMMER BROTHERS FINE PRINTING & LITHOGRAPHY
MEMPHIS, TN. 38101

Printers and Publishers of Cookbooks of Distinction

spreads

NOTES

CHEESE BALL

¼ lb. butter (softened)
8 ounces cream cheese (softened)
1 jar Kraft Old English Cheese
1 jar Roka Blue Cheese
1 jar Kraft Garlic Cheese
dash Worcestershire
1 T minced chives or parsley (optional)

Cream ingredients together well. Chill slightly. Form into three balls and chill 4 or 5 hours. To serve, roll in chopped pecans. Serve with crackers. These can be frozen.

CHEESE BALL

1 lb. Cheddar cheese   4 garlic buds
1 lb. sharp cheese   1 small package blue cheese
1 large cream cheese   3 dashes Tabasco

Let cheese get to room temperature. Mix thoroughly. Make in balls or rolls and cover in ground pecans.

CHEESE BALL

1 lb. mild Cheddar cheese   1 clove minced garlic
8 ounces cream cheese   2 T grated onion

Soften cheese and grate Cheddar. Add garlic and onion. Shape into ball and chill. Roll in parsley or pecans.

spreads

CHEESE AND SALTED ALMOND SANDWICHES

1 C grated American cheese
¼ C chopped salted almonds
2 T mayonnaise

Combine all ingredients for filling.

CHERRY-NUT SANDWICH SPREAD

8 ounces cream cheese
4 T finely chopped Maraschino cherries
cherry juice
½ C chopped nuts
1 T mayonnaise

Mix softened cream cheese with cherry juice and mayonnaise. Add cherries and nuts, mixing well.

CHRISTMAS CHEESE BALL

3 packages blue cheese
  (2 ounce size)
2 packages cream cheese
  (3 ounce size)
½ lb. New York sharp cheese
½ C nuts, chopped fine

1 T Worcestershire
1 T crushed onion
1 t chili sauce
½ C fresh parsley

Let cheese sit at room temperature for 2 hours. Mix in mixer. Add seasoning. Roll into two balls. Spread nuts and parsley over balls. Refrigerate until ready to serve.

COCKTAIL SANDWICHES

3 hard-boiled eggs
18 small stuffed olives
2 thin slices Bermuda
   onions

1 T mustard
salt and pepper to taste
thin bread or crackers

Chop and then grind into paste the eggs, olives, and onions. Blend in mustard and salt to taste. Sprinkle in small amount of pepper. Spread on very thin sliced bread or crackers. Also makes a good filling for a closed sandwich garnished with lettuce.

CUCUMBER NUT ROLL

8 ounces cream cheese
1 t grated onion

2 t grated cucumber
½ to ¾ C finely chopped
   pecans

Cream together cheese, onion, and cucumber. Form into tiny balls and roll in nuts or spread on finger sandwiches after adding nuts.

DEVILED CHEESE SANDWICHES

½ lb. cream cheese
1 small onion
3 canned pimentos
2 hard boiled eggs, chopped

¼ t salt
½ t paprika
4 T mayonnaise

Combine the cheese, onion, and pimento. Add the chopped eggs, seasoning, mayonnaise and mix well.

spreads

EASY SHRIMP SANDWICHES

8 ounces cream cheese   garlic powder
1 small can shrimp   mayonnaise
Worcestershire

Combine ingredients. Spread on bread or crackers.

EGG SALAD ROLL-UPS

6 hard-boiled eggs   1 medium onion, minced
6 T mayonnaise   1 t curry powder
6 T chopped celery   12-18 slices soft white bread

Finely chop hard-cooked eggs, add mayonnaise, celery, onion, and curry. Mix well. Remove crusts from bread slices; spread with egg mixture. Roll up jelly roll fashion; fasten edges together with toothpicks. Cover with damp cloth; place in refrigerator to chill. Just before serving cut in one inch slices.

FILLING FOR CRAB CANAPES

1 C drained crabmeat   mayonnaise
1/8 t lemon juice   drained capers (small
    amount)

Combine ingredients with enough mayonnaise to hold together.

GARLIC CHEESE ROLL

8 ounces grated American cheese (or one small box Velveeta)
3 ounces cream cheese

½ C chopped pecans
chili powder
¼ t garlic salt (or less)

Have cheese at room temperature. Blend well. Add garlic salt and pecans. Form into a roll as desired. Coat outside of roll with chili powder. Chill in refrigerator. Will keep several weeks.

HOT PEPPER JELLY

¾ C hot pepper
1 C bell pepper
1½ C cider vinegar

6½ C sugar
1½ bottle Certo
food coloring

Chop peppers in blender. Boil vinegar and sugar 3 or 4 minutes. Add Certo, pepper, and food coloring. Simmer 5 minutes until transparent. Pour into sterilized jars. Serve over block of cream cheese with Melba rounds.

LEMON CHEESE SANDWICH FILLING

3 T lemon juice
½ C sugar
¼ C nuts

1 t lemon rind
4 egg yolks, beaten
2 T mayonnaise

Cook ingredients until thick. Add nuts and mayonnaise. Spread on open face sandwiches.

LOBSTER RIBBON SANDWICHES

Chop cooked lobster meat, frozen or canned, very fine. Add 2 or 3 chopped hard-boiled eggs, several tablespoons mayonnaise, and season with grated onion, salt and pepper.

Mash yolks of 4 hard-boiled eggs through a sieve and work to a paste with one small package cream cheese and 1 teaspoon anchovy paste. Season with 2 tablespoons lemon juice, 1 teaspoon Worcestershire, ¼ teaspoon dry mustard, and a little sugar.

Taste for seasoning. If the mixture is not salty enough, add more anchovy paste.

Make four-decker sandwiches, top and bottom layers lobster and center layer eggs. These may be frozen and served later.

OLIVE AND CRABMEAT SANDWICHES

1 can (6½ ounces) crab meat, drained and flaked
1½ C grated mild Chedder cheese
1 T instant minced onion
1/3 C sliced pimento stuffed olives
1 C sour cream
12 slices rye bread

Mix all ingredients, except bread, and spread bread slices with mixture. Cut into tiny sandwiches and sprinkle with paprika or parsley.

PARTY RYE SANDWICHES

3 ounces cream cheese   **chopped black olives**
1 hard-boiled egg   **dash Worcestershire**
chopped onion   **salt and pepper**
chopped cherry pepper

Mash egg while warm into cream cheese. Add rest of ingredients and spread on small party rye bread.

PEG ADDY'S CUCUMBER SANDWICHES

2 large packages cream cheese, softened
½ grated cucumber (use only drained pulp)
½ grated small onion (only pulp)
3 shakes Tabasco
½ t salt
pepper to taste
½ t lemon juice

Combine ingredients. If too stiff, add small amount of mayonnaise and blend in mixer. Chill overnight before using. A few drops of green food coloring may also be added. This freezes well.

PINEAPPLE CHEESE BALL

2 large packages cream cheese
1 can 8½ ounces crushed pineapple, drained
2 C pecans, crushed
¼ C chopped green pepper
2 T chopped onions
1 T seasoned salt

Mix together and refrigerate. Roll in 1 cup chopped pecans before serving.

SALMON PARTY LOG

2 C salmon (1 lb. can)   ¼ t salt
8 ounces cream cheese,   ¼ t liquid smoke
  softened   ½ C chopped pecans
1 T lemon juice   3 T snipped parsley
2 t grated onion
1 t prepared horesradish

Drain and flake salmon, removing skin and bones. Combine salmon with next six ingredients; mix thoroughly. Chill several hours. Combine pecans and parsley. Shape salmon mixture into 8 by 2 inch log; roll in nut mixture; chill well. Serve with crackers.

spreads

SANDWICH OR CRACKER SPREAD

1 lb. carrots
½ C celery, chopped fine
1 C finely ground nuts
½ C India Relish

garlic salt or juice to taste
juice of one lemon
one pint of mayonnaise

Grind or grate finely carrots. Press out juice well. Mix other ingredients and serve on crackers. Tiny sandwiches can also be made with this spread.

SANDWICH OR CRACKER SPREAD

8 ounces cream cheese, softened
4 T butter or margarine, softened
½ C sour cream

1 T snipped parsley
1 t steak sauce
one 7 ¾ ounce can salmon

Beat cream cheese, butter, and sour cream till fluffy. Add parsley, steak sauce, and salmon, (drained). Chill.

SAVORY HAM SPREAD

3 lbs. canned ham, ground (7 cups)
¾ C mayonnaise
½ C sweet pickles, chopped fine

1/3 C chopped parsley
1/3 C cut sweet pepper (or pepper relish)

Combine ingredients. Pack into mold and refrigerate. Unmold and garnish.

SHRIMP PASTE

1 lb. cooked shrimp	1/3 C blue cheese, crumbled
1 C mayonnaise	2 to 3 t fresh lemon juice
1 T horseradish	1 t Worcestershire
hot sauce to taste	

Grind shrimp and blue cheese together, using fine blade of grinder. Add remaining ingredients and chill. Garnish with chopped parsley.

SHRIMP SANDWICHES

Clean and boil 1½ pounds shrimp. Grind with medium onion. Add salt, lemon juice, and red pepper to taste. Soften to spreading consistency with mayonnaise. Spread on small rounds of bread.

SMOKED OYSTER ROLL

1 can smoked oysters	dash of Accent in cheese
¾ C chopped pecans	¼ t Beau Monde seasoning
2 T sour cream	2 T mayonnaise
8 ounces cream cheese	

Blend cheese, seasoning, and mayonnaise. Roll out on waxed paper about 4 inches wide and ½ inches thick. Sprinkle nuts and oysters over cheese. Roll as jelly roll and place in refrigerator. Use as spread for crackers.

VERSATILE VEGETABLE SPREAD

1 carton cottage cheese
1 package frozen chopped spinach
1 pimento, chopped
2 or 3 spring onions, chopped
small amount of mayonnaise (optional)
salt, red pepper or Tabasco

Bring spinach barely to a boil, break apart with a fork. Drain and thoroughly squeeze all water out. Mix with other ingredients.

Other additions: chopped green pepper, chopped celery, chopped olives, grated carrots.

WALNUT-CRAB CRACKER SPREAD

1 (7½ ounce) can crabmeat, minced and well drained
2 (8 ounce) packages cream cheese, softened
2 T lemon juice
1¼ C walnuts, chopped
salt or garlic salt to taste
2 T onion, chopped fine

Combine crab and cheese. Blend in onion, lemon juice and salt. Add ½ cup walnuts, mixing well. Turn mixture out on foil, shaping into four logs. Roll into remaining nuts till surface is well coated. Chill until firm. This freezes very well and recipe makes enough for two boxes crackers.

NOTES

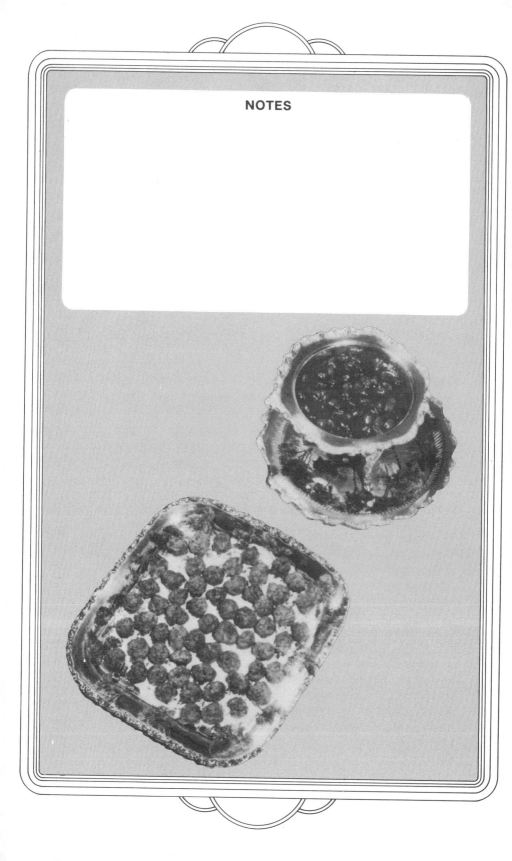

ARTICHOKES AND HAM

Cut thin sliced ham into strips. Use marinated quartered artichoke hearts. Wrap each one in a piece of ham and secure with a pick. Place in a baking dish. Pour oil over the artichoke hearts.
Heat in 325° oven for fifteen - twenty minutes. Serve hot.

ASPARAGUS SPEARS ROLLED IN HAM

18 canned asparagus spears
¾ C salad oil
¼ C wine vinegar
¼ t salt

½ t dried basil
freshly ground black pepper
9 slices of thin boiled or baked ham

Marinate asparagus in oil, vinegar, salt, pepper, and basil for 2 hours. Drain thoroughly. Cut ham in half crosswise and wrap around asparagus spear securing with a wooden pick. May be prepared ahead of time. Yield - 6 servings.

BACON ROLL-UPS

¼ C butter
½ C water
1½ C herb-seasoned
   stuffing

1 egg, slightly beaten
1/4 lb. hot pork sausage
2/3 lb. sliced bacon

Melt butter in water. Remove from heat, stir in stuffing, then egg and sausage. Blend thoroughly. Chill for an hour. Shape into small balls. Cut bacon strips into thirds crosswise. Wrap bacon around dressing mixture and fasten with toothpick. Place on rack in shallow pan and bake 375° for 35 minutes or until brown and crisp. Drain on paper towel and serve hot. May be made ahead of time and frozen before baking. Yield - 36 appetizers.

BARBECUED CHICKEN WINGS

2 - 3 lb. chicken wings,
  cut up (throw away tips)
1 C soy sauce
3 t sugar or ¼ C pineapple
  syrup
¼ C white wine
2 cloves garlic, mashed or
  sprinkle wings generously
  with garlic powder

¼ C Mazola oil
1 t Accent
1 t (level) ground
  ginger

Marinate for 16 hours. Bake at 325° for 1 ½ to 2 hours. Sauce may be saved in refrigerator and used again.

BARBECUED PORK RIBLETS

Combine ½ C each lemon juice and olive oil, 1/3 C sliced scallions, ¼ C cream sherry, 3 t lemon rind, 1 t salt, ½ t crushed red pepper and 1 clove crushed garlic. Pour over 1 ½ lbs. pork riblets and let marinate overnight. Bake 30 minutes at 375°.

BITE SIZE PIZZAS

Sausage (patty type)
1 small can tomato paste
1 small can tomato sauce
French bread

Mix first three ingredients and put in the refrigerator with one clove of garlic. Cover and let stand overnight.
Cut French bread very thin. Spread with mixture, sprinkle with Parmesan cheese. Bake at 450° until brown.

CHICKEN AND ALMONDS IN PUFF SHELLS

1 C chopped cooked chicken
¼ C finely chopped celery
¼ C chopped blanched almonds
Enough mayonnaise to moisten
Salt, pepper, and lemon juice to taste.

Mix above ingredients together and fill cream puff shells. Cream Puff Shell - ¼ C boiling water, ¼ C butter, ½ C flour, and 2 unbeaten eggs. Melt butter in water. Add flour all at once and stir vigorously. When a ball forms in the center of the pan, remove from the heat and cool 5 minutes. Add 1 egg and mix thoroughly by hand or mixer. Add second egg and repeat beating. Drop 1 teaspoon at a time, 2 inches apart, on a buttered cookie sheet. Bake at 375° till brown or until all beads of moisture have disappeared (about 25 minutes). Take one shell out and test it. If it doesn't fall puffs are done. When cool fill with mixture.

CHICKEN DRUMETTE

Take drumettes from 12 chicken wings, dip in milk, dust with mixture of ¼ C flour and ¼ t salt. Saute in ¼ C olive oil with 2 or 3 crushed cloves of garlic. Remove and sprinkle with minced parsley or toasted sesame seeds.

CHICKEN FINGER LOGS

1 3-oz. pkg. of cream cheese
2 C ground cooked chicken
Chicken broth
1 loaf sliced bread
butter or margarine

Soften cream cheese; add chicken and enough broth to make spreading consistency. Trim crusts from bread; roll each slice thin with a rolling pin. Spread bread with butter and chicken mixture; roll as for a jelly roll. Place on baking sheet. Bake at 400° till browned. Serve hot.

CHICKEN LIVERS

2 lb. chicken livers   1 T vinegar
¼ C soy sauce   ¼ t pepper
¼ C salad oil   2 cloves garlic, crushed
2 T catsup

Cut livers in ½ and marinate overnight. Roll liver in brown sugar and wrap in ½ slice of bacon. Broil on both sides.

CHINESE SPARERIBS

4 lbs. spareribs   1 T sugar
1 C soy sauce (Kikkoman)   1 t salt
½ C water   1 clove of garlic, minced.
3 T red wine

Score meat between ribs, but not all the way through. Combine ingredients and pour over the meat. Let stand an hour or so, turning once. Place on grill over medium coals, cooking and basting for 1 ½ hours or bake in 350° oven for 1 ½ hours. 20 - 30 appetizers.

CHOPPED LIVER

1 lb. chicken livers   3 hard cooked eggs
2 to 4 T chicken fat   1 t salt
1 or 2 onions, diced fine   ¼ t pepper

Saute onions in fat in skillet. Reserve the onions and saute liver in the remaining fat. Grind, chop or blend the liver, onions and eggs to a smooth paste. Add salt and pepper. May add additional finely chopped raw onion to the mixture. Serve as a spread for crackers or on lettuce as an appetizer or stuff celery.

COCKTAIL MEATBALLS

2 lbs. hamburger	2 C bread crumbs
1 lb. ground pork	8 eggs
2 T salt	½ pint olive oil
½ T pepper	

Combine all ingredients. Shape into meatballs. Don't worry about the consistency as they will shape well. Add meatballs to Cocktail Meatball Sauce and cook for 1 hour over low heat.

Cocktail Meatball Sauce:	2 cans tomato juice (4 cups)
½ T paprika	3 (# 2) cans of tomatoes
1 C sugar	4 onions, finely sliced
1 T chili powder	1 clove garlic
5 t salt	4 T flour
½ T pepper	

Combine all ingredients in large kettle and cover. Cook approximately 2 hours, then add meatballs.

COCKTAIL WEINERS

Mix one 6 - ounce jar (¾ Cup) prepared mustard and one 10 oz. jar (1 cup) currant jelly in chafing dish or saucepan over low heat. Slice 1 lb. frankfurters diagonally in bite size pieces.

CRABAPPLE TIDBITS

Spiced crabapples
Cocktail sausages

Preheat oven to 400°. Core crabapples and insert cocktail sausage into space. Heat at 400° degrees for 5 minutes.

CRESCENT FRANKS

Cut each triangle in half from one can Italian - flavored crescent rolls. Spread with mustard and drained sauerkraut. Roll up 16 cocktail franks in dough. Bake 375° for 15 minutes.

DRIED BEEF ROLLS

1 jar dried beef
1 pkg. cream cheese

onion, finely chopped
2 or 3 drops of green food
coloring

Soften cream cheese and mix in other ingredients. Spread on slices of beef. Roll up and refrigerate. Slice into bite size pieces and serve cold.

EMPANADITAS

Filling:
½ lb. ground beef
½ green pepper, chopped
1 onion, chopped
1 8-oz. tomato sauce
¼ t garlic powder

1 t salt
dash Tabasco
¼ t steak sauce

Cook beef, pepper and onion in heavy skillet, do not brown. Add rest of ingredients, simmer for 25 minutes.

Pastry: pie crust mix (can add dash of Tabasco). Roll thin and cut in circles. (1 ½" rounds). Place 1 t filling and top with another circle. Dampen edges and fold over half of circle. Seal edges by indenting with work tines. Brush with beaten egg (put olive slice on top).

Bake at 425° or fry in deep fat 15 minutes.

EXTRA-ORDINARY MEATBALLS

4 lbs. ground beef
1 egg, slightly beaten
1 large onion, grated
salt

1 12-oz. bottle chili sauce
1 12-oz. jar grape jelly
juice of one lemon

Blend together meat, eggs, onion and salt. Form into 100 meatballs. Combine jelly, chili sauce and lemon juice. Pour over meatballs and simmer one hour. Serve in heated chafing dish.

HAM PUFFS

Blend:
8-oz. cream cheese
1 beaten egg yolk
1 t onion juice
½ t baking powder

salt to taste
¼ t horseradish
¼ t hot sauce

Spread 24 small bread squares with 2-2½ oz. cans of deviled ham. Top with mound of cheese. Bake on cookie sheet at 375° for 10-12 mins.

LITTLE PIZZAS

1 can refrigerator biscuits
1 small can tomato sauce
1 lb. ground beef, cooked
1 t salt

½ t pepper
½ C chopped onions
½ C parmesan cheese

Roll biscuits out to ¼ inch thickness. Spread half the tomato sauce over biscuits. Cover with a layer of beef, sprinkle seasonings and onions and cheese over beef. Top with remaining tomato sauce. Place on greased cookie sheet. Bake 20 minutes.

LUAU BITES

Cut 10 canned water chestnuts in half. Quarter 5 chicken livers. Wrap in ½ slice of bacon and fasten with toothpicks. Marinate in mixture of ¼ C soy sauce, 2 T brown sugar about 4 hours. Drain. Place on broiler rack. Broil 3" from heat till bacon is crisp, turning once.

MARINATED FLANK STEAK

2 C chopped onions	½ t thyme
1 C salad oil	½ t marjoram
2/3 C vinegar	dash pepper
3 or 4 cloves garlic	2 whole flank steaks
2 t salt	Adolph's meat tenderizer

Cut flank steak on bias (where scored) in ½" strips - Use Adolph's liberally - then roll in pinwheels and secure with toothpicks. Cover with onions in a baking dish. Mix all other ingredients and pour slowly on pinwheels. Marinate overnight or longer. Cook on grill and serve. (May put pinwheels on skewers).

MARINATED FLANK STEAK

1/3 C soy sauce	1/8 t garlic salt
1/3 cup cooking oil	1 T minced dry onion
3 T Burgundy wine	3 lb. steak

Marinate at least 4 hours. Cook on grill. Slice thin and serve.

MEAT PATTIES IN SWEET AND SOUR SAUCE

2 C bread crumbs	1 C sliced onion
¼ C chopped onion	1/3 C brown sugar
1 t salt	1 T flour
1/8 t thyme	¼ C vinegar
½ C water	2 T water
1 lb. ground beef	2 t prepared mustard

Combine crumbs, chopped onion, seasonings in ½ C water. Let stand 5 minutes. Mix in meat. Shape into patties. Brown in small amount of fat. In another pan combine rest of ingredients. Pour over meat. Cover and simmer for 35 minutes. Serve hot in chafing dish.

OPEN-FACE HOT DOG REUBEN

12 frankfurters	1 I lb. can sauerkraut, drained
2 T butter or margarine	8 thin slices Swiss Cheese
8 slices of rye bread	½ C mayonnaise or salad
Prepared mustard	dressing
3 T Durkee's sauce	

Split frankfurters in half - lengthwise; brown in skillet in margarine. Mix mustard, mayonnaise and Durkee's together - Spread on each piece of bread on 1 side. Place sauerkraut on each piece of bread; top with 3 frankfurter halves and put thin slice of cheese on top. Broil until cheese is melted. Makes 8 open-face sandwiches. (You may add another piece of bread per sandwich after broiling and toast, giving 8 closed sandwiches).

OVER THE COALS CORNED BEEF

5 lbs. corned beef brisket 2 T brown sugar
1 med. size onion, sliced   ¼ t nutmeg
1 T mixed pickling spices   ⅛ t freshly ground pepper
¼ C prepared mustard

Simmer corned beef in sack with onion and pickling spices in water to cover in a kettle 4 hours or until tender. Let stand in broth until ready to glaze. Brush meat over with about half of the mustard. Mix remaining mustard with brown sugar, nutmeg and pepper in a cup - save for next step. Place meat on grill over hot coals. Grill 15 mins. Turn. Grill 15 mins. longer. Brush half of the mustard mixture over meat. Turn again and grill 15 mins. Brush with remaining mustard mixture - turn again. Grill 15 mins. longer or until crusty brown. Remove meat to cutting board. Slice thin and across the grain.

QUICK FRANK FONDUE

20 cocktail franks   Cooking oil
1 C (8-oz.) refrigerator
  biscuit dough
Barbecue sauce

Pour oil into fondue cooker to no more than ½ capacity. Preheat 10-15 mins. Slash length of franks just deep enough to puncture skin - blot with paper towel and set aside. Separate dough into 10 equal sections, cut each section in half. Wrap each half section around frank, pinch seams to fasten around frank. Spear appetizer at seam so tines of fork cross seam. Immerse in hot oil until golden brown. Dip in barbecue sauce. Yield - 20 appetizers.

RAW HAMBURGER CANAPES

2 lbs. ground round
2 large onions, cut fine
2 cans Valley brand chili
   peppers, cut fine
juice of 2 large lemons

2 raw eggs
1 t Tabasco sauce
1 t salt
1 t pepper

Spread ground round on dough board or meat paper and add onions, peppers, eggs, lemon juice, Tabasco sauce, salt and pepper. Work thoroughly then put ingredients on serving dish. Let stand 4 hours. Serve with saltine crackers.

SAUERKRAUT BALLS

1 onion, grated
¼ C oleo
1 1/3 C ground ham
½ C flour
¼ C ham broth

1 14-oz. can sauerkraut,
   drained and ground
1 egg, beaten
¼ C milk
corn flake crumbs

Cook onion in oleo until soft, stir in ham, milk and flour. Add broth and sauerkraut. Cook, stirring, 5 minutes. Shape in small balls, roll in flour, then egg, then crumbs. Fry in deep fat until brown. Serve warm with hot mustard.

SAUSAGE BALLS

3 C biscuit mix
1 ½ C sharp Cheddar cheese, grated
1 lb. hot bulk sausage

Mix above together and roll into small balls. Bake at 350° for 10-12 mins.

SAUSAGE BALLS

1½ C sifted regular flour	2 C shredded cheese
2 t curry	½ C butter
1 t paprika	1 lb. sausage
¼ t salt	

Up to one week before: In large bowl mix flour, curry, paprika, salt and cheese. With pastry blender cut in butter until mixture is coarse crumbs, shape into a ball, cover and refrigerate.

Meanwhile shape heaping teaspoon sausage meat into small ball. Fry. Divide dough into as many pieces as sausage balls. Shape dough around balls. Wrap and freeze.

At serving time: preheat oven to 400°. Place frozen balls on cookie sheet and bake 12-15 mins. until golden brown.

SAUSAGE ROLLS

2 C flour	5 T shortening
½ t salt	2/3 C milk
3 t baking powder	1 lb. well seasoned sausage

Sift flour, salt and baking powder, cut in shortening. Stir in milk. Halve dough, roll out each half ¼ in. thick on a floured board. Spread with sausage; roll as for jelly roll. Wrap in waxed paper, chill. When ready to serve slice ¼" thick. Bake 5-10 mins. at 400°. Serves 20.

SAUSAGE SWIRLS

1 lb. highly seasoned sausage
1 pkg. of short biscuit dough (roll out to thickness of 1¼ inch)

Spread sausage evenly over biscuit dough. Roll dough over and over and moisten end and seal firmly. Wrap in waxed paper and chill thoroughly. Slice and broil.

STEAK BITES

3 to 4 lbs. round steak,
   cut one inch thick
seasoned instant meat
   tenderizer
1 C red wine
1 garlic clove, crushed
½ C butter

1 T dry mustard
1 t Worcestershire
dash pepper
few drops Tabasco

Apply tenderizer to steak as label directs about 2 hrs. before serving. In large pan, mix wine and garlic. Add steak and cover. Place in refrigerator for 1½ hours, turning once.

Broil steak till medium rare - about fifteen minutes, turning once. Meanwhile in a medium saucepan melt butter, add remaining ingredients and 2 T marinade from steak. Cut steak into cubes and put into chafing dish; pour on sauce and serve at once with cocktail picks.

SUGAR GLAZED BACON CURLS

Roll 1 lb. sliced bacon in light brown sugar. Lay slices on a jelly roll pan; bake at 300° till bacon is browned and glazed, about 30-40 mins. Roll on fork into curls while still hot.

SURPRISE BALLS

1 lb. ground beef
1 small can of deviled ham
Roquefort or blue cheese

dry red wine
pepper
butter

Mix beef and ham spread together. Add salt and pepper to taste. Cut cheese into small squares and mold meat around them. Place in a bowl and cover with the wine. Let stand for 3 hrs. Drain and pan fry the meat patties. Remove and serve while very hot.

SWEET AND SOUR CHICKEN WINGS

Chicken Wings	1 chopped onion
3 T flour	½ C ketchup
½ t salt	½ C wine vinegar
dash pepper	garlic salt
¼ C shortening	small can crushed pineapple
green pepper, chopped	¼ C brown sugar

Chop vegetables. Flour, then brown chicken in shortening. Put vegetables in and brown. Mix catsup with vinegar, stir in pineapple and brown sugar. Cover and simmer 10 mins. Add chicken; simmer till heated thoroughly. Serve in chafing dish.

SWEET AND SOUR MEATBALLS

Meatballs:

Mix- 1 lb. ground chuck	1 C water chestnuts, sliced
1 ½ t salt	thin or chopped
¼ t pepper	

Mix. Roll in flour, brown in fat and drain.

Sauce:

2 T cornstarch	green pepper, chopped large
½ C sugar	1 can (2 C) pineapple
½ C vinegar	cubes and juice
1 T soy sauce	

Combine. Bring to a boil, lower heat and cook 5 minutes. Pour over meatballs. Serve hot with toothpicks. Note: Meatballs may be frozen but not in sauce.

SWEET AND SOUR MEATBALLS
WITH PINEAPPLE AND PEPPERS

3 large green peppers, cut
into 12-15 strips
1 lb. ground beef

1 egg
4 T cornstarch
1 t salt
2 T onion, chopped fine
few grains of pepper

1 C pineapple juice

4 slices of pineapple, cut in
pieces
1 T soy sauce
3 T vinegar
6 T water
½ C sugar
1 T oil

Mix beef, egg, 1 T cornstarch, salt, onion and pepper; form into 18 balls or more. Brown them in a small amount of oil (¾ C). Drain. To 1 T oil add pineapple juice and cook over low heat. Add mixture of 3 T cornstarch, soy sauce, vinegar, water and sugar. Cook until juice thickens, stirring constantly. Add meatballs, pineapple and peppers. Heat thoroughly.

TERIYAKI MINIATURES

1 T soy sauce
2 t sugar
¼ t instant minced onion
dash garlic salt

dash of ground ginger
½ lb. lean ground beef
½ C fine soft bread crumbs

Combine soy sauce, 1 T water, sugar, onion, garlic salt and ginger. Let stand 10 mins. Mix meat and crumbs, stir in soy mixture. Shape into ¾ inch meatballs. Refrigerate till serving time. Spear on fondue forks. Cook in deep hot fat 375° in fondue pot about 1½ mins. Serve with heated catsup and mustard for dunking. Makes 30 meatballs.

WHISKY WEINERS

¾ C catsup, or chili sauce   3 oz. bourbon
¼ C brown sugar   juice of ½ lemon
1 T onion, grated

Mix and boil with 1 lb. beef weiners cut in 1 inch long pieces or cocktail weiners. Cook slowly 30 mins. on stove and serve in heated chafing dish.

YUMMY TURNOVERS

Filling:
1 pkg. dry mushroom   1½ C diced water chestnuts
   soup mix   2 T chopped onion
½ lb. ground round
   (or more)
1 C drained bean sprouts

Brown meat. Drain well. Stir in other ingredients.
Pastry: 4 cans of crescent rolls. Roll out dough. Wrap tiny bits of filling in pastry. Bake 350° for 20 mins. or until lightly browned.

sweets

NOTES

BANANA BREAD

2 eggs	1¾ C sifted, all purpose flour
1/3 C soft shortening	¾ t soda
2 ripe bananas, peeled and sliced	1¼ t cream of tartar
	½ t salt
2/3 C sugar	

Preheat oven 350°F. Grease 8x4 inch loaf pan. Combine eggs, shortening, bananas and sugar in glass container of blender. Cover and blend until smooth, about 30 seconds. Sift dry ingredients together into mixing bowl. Pour blender combination over dry in-gredients. Stir only until combined. Pour into greased loaf pan. Bake about 45 minutes or until lightly browned. Turn out to cool on wire rack. When cool, wrap in waxed paper and chill several hours or over night before slicing. Makes one loaf. Excellent sliced thinly into squares and served with cream cheese.

BANANA BREAD

2/3 C sugar	3 T sour milk
1/3 C soft shortening	1 C mashed bananas
2 eggs	2 C flour
½ t soda	1 t baking powder
½ t salt	½ C chopped pecans

Mix together sugar, shortening and eggs. Stir in milk and bananas. Sift together flour, baking powder, soda and salt. Mix all together. Blend in nuts. Pour into well greased 9x5x3" loaf pan. Let stand 20 min. before baking. Bake at 350° for 50 to 60 min.

sweets

BANANA MUFFINS

½ C shortening	2½ C flour
1 C sugar	2½ t soda
1 C mashed bananas	½ t salt
2 eggs, lightly beaten	

Cream shortening with sugar in a bowl and add bananas. Add the eggs and mix well. Sift dry ingredients together and stir into batter. Pour into tiny greased muffin tins. Bake at 350° for 15 min.

BOURBON BALLS

3 C finely rolled vanilla wafers	1½ C finely chopped nuts
1 C powdered sugar	3 T corn syrup
1 ½ T cocoa	1½ C bourbon

Mix together, shape into 1 inch balls and roll in powdered sugar. Eat immediately or store in tight container.

CHOCOLATE COVERED PEANUT BUTTER BALLS

1 C chopped nuts	½ C cornflake crumbs
1 C chopped dates	1 C powdered sugar
1 C peanut butter	

Mix together and roll into balls the size of a walnut and refrigerate 1 hour.

Chocolate coating:

1 8-oz. bar milk chocolate	½ bar paraffin
½ pkg. chocolate chips	

Melt chocolate and wax in separate containers. Pour wax into chocolate and put into double boiler to maintain spreading consistency. Drop in balls, roll and take out with a toothpick. Chocolate will harden and form coating.

CHOCOLATE MERINGUES

2 eggs whites   1 t vanilla
½ t cream of tartar   ½ t salt

Combine and beat until soft peaks form. Add ¾ C sugar. Beat until stiff. Add 1 pkg. chocolate chips and ½ C chopped nuts. Drop by tsp. onto cookie sheet covered with tinfoil. Cook 300° for 25 min.

CHOCOLATE REFRIGERATOR CUPCAKES

1 stick margarine   1 t vanilla
1½ of 1 oz. squares   2 eggs, well beaten
   bitter chocolate   1 C chopped nuts
1 C sugar
2/3 C unsifted flour

ICING

2 T margarine
1 oz. square bitter chocolate
¾ box powdered sugar
cold coffee

Directions for cupcakes: Melt butter and chocolate together in double boiler. Mix other ingredients, add to chocolate butter mixture. Place small size paper baking cups in muffin tins. Fill half full, no more. Bake 12 min. The cakes may not look done but do not over cook.

Directions for Icing: Melt butter and chocolate. Add powdered sugar gradually and enough cold coffee to make smooth mixture. Top hot cupcakes. Put in refrigerator or freeze.

COCONUT MERINGUE CUPCAKES

3 egg whites	½ t almond extract
¼ t cream of tartar	6 T all purpose flour
2/3 C sugar	1 (3½ oz.) can coconut

Beat egg whites and cream of tartar till frothy. Gradually add sugar and beat till sugar is thoroughly blended. Add almond extract, then flour, sprinkling a little at a time on the meringue, beating at low speed only until flour is blended. Fold in coconut. Fill almost to top. Bake at 325° for 30 min. or till golden brown. Freezes well. Makes 12 large muffins or 24 tiny muffins. Perfect for teas.

COCONUT SNACK BALLS

1 pkg. (3 oz.) softened cream cheese
1 t each grated lemon and orange peel or more to suit taste
2 t finely chopped nuts
Toasted flaked coconut

Blend softened cream cheese, orange and lemon peels and nuts. Form into small balls and roll in coconut. Chill before serving.

CRANBERRY CONFECTION CUPCAKES

¾ C plain flour	3½ C chopped nuts
½ t baking powder	2 eggs
½ t salt	1 t lemon extract
2 C fresh cranberries	¾ C sugar
1 pkg. (8 oz.) pitted chopped dates	

Sift baking powder, salt and flour together. Combine dates, cranberries, pecans with mixture in large bowl, toss together till fruit is evenly coated. Beat eggs and sugar till light and fluffy. Add extract. Pour over flour fruit mixture. Mix thoroughly. Line muffin tins with paper liners. Pack fruit till 2/3 full. Bake 300° 40-50 min. or till cake tests done. Cook in pan 15 min.

CRESCENTS

1 C butter (2 sticks)	2 t vanilla extract
4 t powdered sugar	2 T water (add gradually)
2 C plain flour (measure after sifting)	1 C nuts

Mix together all ingredients except sugar. Shape into crescents. Bake at 325°. While hot, roll in powdered sugar.

DATE MUFFINS

1 egg, beaten separately	pinch of salt
2 T sugar	1½ C milk
2 C flour	2 T melted butter
2 t baking powder	1 C dates, cut in small pieces

Mix. Bake 15 min. in hot oven; in small buttered tins. Makes 30.

sweets

DATE AND NUT BREAD

2 pkg. dates	4 C nuts
1 C flour	1 C sugar
Vanilla	3 eggs

Beat eggs. Add sugar, flour, nuts, dates, and vanilla. Bake at 325° about 1 hour.

DATE TARTS

Crust: Make favorite pie crust recipe or use a mix. Roll out and cut with scalloped cookie cutter to fit into tassie pans. Bake.

Filling:

4 eggs	1 stick butter, melted
1 C sugar	1 pkg. (8 oz.) chopped dates

Beat eggs well, add sugar, butter, and dates. Cook in double boiler till thick. Add ¾-1 C sherry and 1 C chopped nuts. Spoon filling into pastry shells and dot with whipped cream. The filling fills about 75 shells.

EASY PARTY MINTS

3 C powdered sugar
1 C boiling water

Mix powdered sugar and boiling water. Cook to soft ball stage. Add green or red food coloring and peppermint extract to suit taste. Beat till thickened. Drop onto waxed paper. If mixture becomes too thick to drop, put back over heat for a minute.

FROSTED GRAPES OR STRAWBERRIES

1 egg white
grapes or strawberries
sugar

Brush fruit with slightly beaten egg white; sprinkle with sugar. Let dry individually on wire racks.

FRUIT CAKE COOKIES

1 lb. margarine	2 t cinnamon
1½ C sugar	6 C flour
1½ C brown sugar	2 t soda
3 eggs	1 C chopped nuts
2 t vanilla	1 small bottle cherries

Mix ingredients together and chill for 2 or 3 hours. Then make into rolls. Keep in freezer until ready to cook. Slice and bake at 375°. You can use glazed cherries also.

sweets

FUDGE CAKE SQUARES

½ C margarine
2 T cocoa
2 eggs
1 C sugar

¾ C sifted plain flour
½ t salt
1 t vanilla
1 C chopped nuts
16 large marshmallows

Melt butter, blend in cocoa. Beat eggs, add sugar and beat. Stir into butter-cocoa mixture. Add flour and salt. Mix well. Add vanilla and nuts. Stir well. Pour in 8 inch square greased pan and bake 30 min. at 350°. Cut marshmallows into halves and press down on cooked hot brownies. Pour this frosting on top.

Frosting:
2 C confectioners sugar
¼ C cocoa

Heat ¼ C evaporated milk and 2 T butter. Add milk to sugar and cocoa. Beat till smooth. Let brownies cool and cut into squares.

FUDGE NUT BALLS

1 6-oz. pkg. semi-sweet
chocolate pieces
3 T corn syrup
½ C evaporated milk
1 t vanilla

½ C powdered sugar
1C chopped pecans
2½ C crushed
vanilla wafers

Heat chocolate pieces in 2 qt. bowl over boiling water until melted. Remove bowl from water and stir in the corn syrup, milk and vanilla gradually. Add the sugar and mix until smooth. Stir in nuts. Fold in wafer crumbs, about ¼ at a time and mix well. Let stand at room temperature for 30 min. Shape into 1 inch balls and roll balls one at a time, in additional powdered sugar. About 4½ dozen. Chill.

GELATIN STRAWBERRIES

1 15-oz. can sweetened condensed milk
1 lb. coconut, ground (be sure the package is marked fine:
   otherwise you will have to grind it yourself.)
2 3-oz. pkg. strawberry flavored gelatin
1 C finely ground almonds
1 T granulated sugar
1 t vanilla extract
½ t almond extract

Combine condensed milk, coconut, 1 pkg. of the dry gelatin, almonds, sugar and flavorings. Mix well, with hands shape to form strawberries. Roll berries in remaining pkg of gelatin to coat thoroughly. Allow to dry before storing. Use any kind of green tinted frosting piped through a pastry tube to form leaf or stem. Piece of green candied cherry or green tinted almond may be used. Do not have to be refrigerated.

ICE BOX CHEESE WAFERS

½ lb. grated sharp cheese   1½ C sifted flour
¼ lb. butter, creamed   ½ t salt
cayenne pepper as desired

Cream together cheese, butter, salt and pepper. Add flour. Make into roll. Wrap in waxed paper and put in refrigerator. Will keep a month. When needed, slice into thin wafers and bake in moderate oven. A pecan half on each wafer is decorative. 6-8 dozen.

KOLOCKIES (German Cookies)

6 eggs	½ C sugar
1 lb. crisco	1 t salt
1 large can evaporated milk	6 C flour
1 cake fresh yeast	

Mix crisco, sugar, salt and flour. Add eggs one at a time. Add yeast dissolved in milk. Mix together. Let rise in refrigerator over night. In the morning, roll dough thin, parts at a time on sugared and floured board. Cut in 2 or 3 inch squares. Place 1 t of favorite preserves or jelly in the middle of squares. Fold two opposite corners together. Bake in 350° oven till done 25 or 30 min.

LEMON PECAN DAINTIES

2/3 C shortening	1 T lemon peel
1 C sugar	2 C sifted enriched flour
1 well beaten egg	1 t baking powder
1 T lemon juice	1 C pecans

Cream shortening and sugar; add dash salt, egg, lemon juice and peel; beat well. Sift dry ingredients and add to mixture. Add nuts. Shape in rolls; chill. 350° 12-15 min.

OLD FASHIONED SOUTHERN TEACAKES

2¼ C sifted flour   1 C sugar
¼ t salt   2 eggs, beaten
2 t baking powder   ½ t vanilla
½ C butter   1 T milk

Sift flour, salt and baking powder together. Cream butter, sugar and eggs. Add vanilla, milk and dry ingredients. Blend well. Place dough on lightly floured board. Sprinkle a little flour over dough and roll out about ½ inch thick. Cut with small cookie or biscuit cutter. Place on greased cookie sheet and bake 350-375° for about 12 to 15 min. or until lightly browned on top.

MYSTERIOUS SQUARES

½ C butter
1 C flour
Cream and spread on 10x12 pan. Bake 12-15 min. 350°.
Beat 2 eggs and add:
½ C coconut
1 C nuts
1½ C brown sugar
1 t vanilla
2 T flour
½ t baking powder
¼ t salt

Spread over cooked butter and flour when cooled. Bake in moderate oven 10 min. Cool and ice with:
1 ½ C powdered sugar
2 T butter
2 t lemon juice
1 t orange juice

PEANUT BUTTER BALLS

2 sticks margarine
1 1/3 C peanut butter
1 box powdered sugar
1 ½ C graham cracker
  crumbs

1 t butternut flavoring
¼ lb. wax
1 8-oz. box
  semi-sweet chocolate

Melt margarine and peanut butter, remove from heat; add sugar, graham cracker crumbs and flavoring. Mix well and cool. Shape into balls. Refrigerate to chill. Melt wax and chocolate together. Roll balls in mixture and cool.

PEANUT BUTTER STICKS

1 C salad oil
1¼ C peanut butter (crunchy)
1 loaf bread (whole wheat is good)

Cut crusts from bread and cut each slice into 6 strips. Toast crusts and strips in oven at 250° for 1 hour. Mix peanut butter and oil together until well blended. Crush only crusts of bread thoroughly with a rolling pin. (or use blender) Dip toasted strips in peanut butter and oil mixture and coat well. Then roll in toasted crumbs. Let peanut butter sticks dry on paper towels for a least 2 hours. Yield: About 100 sticks. Freezes well, too.

PECAN PIE SURPRISE BAR

1 pkg. Pillsbury Yellow cake mix (save 2/3 C)
½ C butter, melted
1 egg
1 C chopped pecans
Filling:
2/3 C reserved cake mix   1 t vanilla
½ C packed brown sugar   3 eggs
1½ C dark corn syrup

Grease bottom and side of 13x9 dish. Save 2/3 C of dry cake mix for filling. Combine remaining cake mix, butter, and 1 egg, mix till crumbly. Press in pan. Bake at 350° for 15-20 min. (until brown). For filling, combine all ingredients and beat 2 minutes. Prepare filling and pour over partially baked crust. Sprinkle with nuts. Return to oven and bake 30 min. Cool and cut into 36 bars.

PECAN ROLLS

1 box powdered sugar   1 t vanilla flavoring
1 7-oz. jar Marshmallow   1 t almond flavoring
    Cream

Mix together and roll into logs of desired length. Freeze overnight.
2 qts. pecans
2 bags Kraft Caramel

Melt caramel in 3 T of water. Roll logs in caramel and then in pecans. Put on waxed paper to cool.

PECAN TARTLETS

Filling:
¾ C light brown sugar   1 t vanilla
1 egg   dash salt
1 T butter   2/3 C chopped pecans
Crust:
1 3-oz. pkg. cream cheese
1 C flour
¼ lb. butter

Cream cheese and butter. Add flour mixing well. With hands work dough around ungreased tins. Combine filling. Bake 350° 25 min. Miniature tartlets may be made in a child's toy muffin tin.

PECAN TARTS

½ C margarine
½ C sugar

Mix above until fluffy. Stir in 2 egg yolks, 1 t almond extract, 2 C sifted flour. Press evenly into muffin cups (about 1 rounded T). Bake 400° 8-10 min.

Filling:

Bring to a boil ½ C margarine, 1/3 C dark Karo syrup, 1 C confectioners sugar. Stir in 1 C chopped pecans. Top with 1 pecan half. Bake 350° for 5 min. in already baked cup.

PLUM COFFEE CAKE

1 ½ C flour	1/3 C butter
½ C sugar	¾ C milk
3 t baking powder	10-12 small purple plums
½ t salt	

Sift dry ingredients together. Cut in butter. Add milk. Spread batter in greased pan. Cut plums in quarters with peel on. Place on top.

Cream together:

1/3 C sugar   ½ t nutmeg   3 T butter

Sprinkle on top. Bake at 375° 45-50 min.

QUICK AND EASY FUDGE

3 squares unsweetened	1 T water
chocolate	3½ C (1 lb.) sifted
4 T butter or margarine	confectioners sugar
½ C Karo syrup (red label)	1/3 C instant nonfat dry milk
1 t vanilla	1 C chopped nuts

Melt chocolate and butter in top of double boiler. Meanwhile, sift together confectioners sugar and instant nonfat dry milk. Stir Karo syrup, vanilla, and water into chocolate-butter mixture. Add sifted sugar mixture one-half at a time. Continue stirring until mixture is well blended and smooth. Remove from heat, stir in nuts. Turn into buttered 8 inch square pan. When cool cut into squares. Make 1¾ pounds of fudge.

sweets

RING-A-LINGS

1 stick butter	dash of salt
3 T Ten (x) sugar	1 t vanilla
1 C sifted plain flour	1 C finely chopped pecans

Cream butter and sugar together. Add sifted flour and salt, one half at a time, to butter mixture. Add nuts and vanilla. Put in refrigerator for several hours. Take teaspoon-size portion and roll in palms of hand. Place on ungreased cookie sheet and indent with finger. Put small amount of green mint jelly or strawberry preserves in indentation. Bake 300° for 20 min. (3 doz.)

SMOOTHEST DIVINITY

Never try to make this on a rainy day or without a candy thermometer.

½ C Karo syrup (red label)	2 large egg whites
2½ C sugar	1 t vanilla
¼ t salt	1 C chopped nuts
½ C water	

Combine first four ingredients in saucepan. Cook over medium heat stirring constantly, until sugar is dissolved. Cook, without stirring, to firm ball stage (248 F.) Be sure to use candy thermometer. Just before syrup reaches 248 F. beat egg whites until stiff not dry. Pour about ½ of the syrup over the egg whites, beating constantly. Cook the remainder of the syrup to soft crack stage (272 F.) Add syrup slowly to first mixture, beating constantly. Continue beating until mixture holds shape. Add vanilla and nuts; drop from spoon onto waxed paper or tin foil. Makes about 1¾ pounds.

SOUR CREAM COFFEE CAKE

1 stick butter
1 C sugar
2 eggs, beaten slightly
1 t soda mixed with 1 C sour
    cream

1½ C plain flour
1½ t baking powder
1 T vanilla

Cream butter, sugar and eggs. Add sour cream with soda and dry ingredients. Mix in the large amount of vanilla. Pour in greased bundt pan with a tube. Sprinkle on a topping made of ¼ C sugar, ½ t cinnamon and ½ C chopped nuts. Dot with extra butter. Bake 45 min. in moderate oven (350°). Open oven door and allow cake to stay in oven till it has cooled. Remove from pan immediately after taking from oven.

SPICED APRICOT BREAD DAINTY SANDWICHES

1½ C dried apricots, diced
1 C sugar
½ t cloves
¼ t ground nutmeg
½ t ground cinnamon
½ t salt
6 T melted butter

1 C water
1 egg, beaten
2 C all-purpose flour
    measured before sifting
1 t soda
1 C chopped pecans
    or walnuts

Combine apricots, sugar, spices, butter and water in saucepan. Cook 5 min. and cool thoroughly. Add beaten egg, then flour sifted with soda. Stir in nuts, mix well and turn into greased 9x5x3 inch loaf pan. Bake at 350° for 1 hour. Freezes beautifully. For a party, chill bread, then slice thinly and make small dainty sandwiches. Fill with cream cheese (softened) flavored with orange juice, or lemon juice. May add chopped nuts or dates.

sweets

SPICED PECANS

2 T cold water	¼ t cinnamon
1 slightly beaten egg white	¼ t cloves
½ C sugar	¼ t allspice
½ t salt	1 C pecan halves

Add water to egg white. Dissolve sugar in egg white mixture. Add salt and spices. Mix well. Dip nuts in mixture. Place nuts, flat side down on greased cookie sheet. Bake at 250° until golden brown, about one hour.

STRUESEL CAKE SQUARES

½ C butter	2 C all purpose flour
1 8-oz. pkg. cream cheese	2 t baking powder
1 C sugar	½ t soda
2 eggs	salt
1 t vanilla	½ C milk
½ t almond extract	

Mix butter, cheese, sugar, eggs, vanilla and almond extract. Sift dry ingredients 3 times. Add dry ingredients alternately with ½ C milk to first mixture. Cook in 13x9x2 inch pan 35-40 min. at 350°. Mix ½ C flour and ½ C sugar. Cut in ¼ C butter. Add ½ C pecans. Sprinkle over top before baking.

TEATIME TASSIES

1 3-oz. pkg. cream cheese
½ C butter or margarine
1 C sifted plain flour

Let cheese and butter soften to room temperature. Stir in flour. Chill slightly about 1 hour. Shape in 2 dozen 1 inch balls. Place in tiny ungreased (1-¾ in.) muffin pans. Press dough on bottom and sides of cups.

Filling:
1 egg	1 t vanilla
¾ C brown sugar	2/3 C broken nuts
dash of salt	1 T butter

Beat together eggs, sugar, butter, vanilla and salt till smooth. Divide half the pecans along pastry lined cups. Add egg mixture and top with remaining pecans. Bake in slow oven 325° for 25 min.

UNCOOKED MINTS

1½ C sifted powdered sugar	½ T butter
1½ T cream	oil of peppermint to taste

Cut butter into sugar with pastry blender or two knives. Add cream gradually. Add peppermint oil, knead; shape in small balls. Flatten with tines of fork. For nut buds: Dry nuts in oven; when cold, put ball on large end of nut and press with fork.

WILLIAMSBURG COOKIES

½ lb. broken pecans
2 egg whites
12 oz. dark brown sugar
(2 cups)

Beat egg whites until stiff. Add sugar gradually. Add pecans. Grease waxed or brown paper in pan. Drop by teaspoonsful on to paper in pan. Bake at 300° until crisp. Take off immediately.

ORANGE COATED PECANS

1½ C sugar
3 T fresh orange juice
1 t orange rind, grated

¼ C water
1 lb. pecan halves (4 cups)

Toast nuts in one tbsp. butter. Place on paper towel to absorb excess moisture. Cook sugar, water and juice until it forms a softball in cold water. Remove from stove; stir until creamy. Add orange rind and nuts. Mix well. Pour out on waxed paper. Separate.

NOTES

ANCHOVY PUFFS

½ C butter or margarine   1 C flour
1 3-oz. pkg. cream cheese   Anchovy paste

Combine butter and cream cheese. Blend in flour. Chill dough thoroughly. Roll dough out thin. Cut with 2-inch cookie cutter. Spread with anchovy paste and fold over. Seal edges with fork and bake at 400° for 10 minutes. May be made ahead and frozen before baking.

CLAM DIP

3 T butter or margarine   4 T ketchup
1 small onion, finely   1 T Worcestershire sauce
  chopped   1 T sherry
½ green pepper,   4 T red pepper or
  finely chopped   Tabasco to taste
2 7½-oz. cans clams,
  drained
½ lb. processed cheese

Melt butter in top of double boiler. Add onion and green pepper and saute until tender (about three minutes). Add remaining ingredients and heat until cheese is melted (stir often). Add more sherry to thin. Add more cheese and clams to thicken. Serve with melba toast.

CRAB PUFFS

1 large pkg. cream cheese	Dash red pepper
1 can crabmeat	Dash mustard
Dash seasoned salt	Dash garlic salt
1 t Worcestershire sauce	Sandwich bread

Mix ingredients until smooth. Cut bread into rounds. Toast one side. Butter other side. Pile crabmeat on buttered side. Cover with crabmeat mixture and heat in oven until mixture bubbles.

CRAB CANAPES

18 thin slices	¼ C ketchup
sandwich bread	1 t grated onion
6 T butter or margarine,	1 t lemon juice, freshly
softened	squeezed
1 6½ - oz. can crabmeat	Capers
drained and flaked	
1 8 - oz. pkg. cream cheese,	
softened	

Cut 5 rounds from each slice of bread with a cookie cutter. Brush one side of rounds with butter. Bake at 400° for about 6 minutes; cool. Combine remaining ingredients except capers. Spread mixture on toasted rounds; garnish with capers. Yield: 90 canapes.

CRABMEAT BACON ROLLS

¼ C tomato juice
1 egg, well beaten
1 7½-oz. can (1 Cup)
  crabmeat, flaked and
  cartilage removed
½ C fine dry bread
  crumbs

1 T snipped parsley
1 T lemon juice
¼ t salt
¼ t Worcestershire sauce
Dash pepper
9 slices bacon, cut in half

Mix tomato juice and egg. Add crabmeat, bread crumbs, parsley, lemon juice and rest of ingredients. Mix thoroughly. Roll into 18 finger shapes about 2 inches long. Wrap each roll spiral fashion with ½ slice of bacon. Fasten with pick. Broil 5 inches from heat about 10 minutes, turning often to brown evenly. Serve hot. Yield: 18 rolls.

CRABMEAT MOLD

2 t unflavored gelatin
¼ C cold water
½ C mayonnaise
2 C crabmeat
Salt, pepper and lemon
  juice to taste

1 C celery, finely chopped
1 T chopped parsley
1 T chopped chives
½ t chopped tarragon or
  ¼ t dried tarragon

Soften gelatin in cold water and dissolve over hot water. Cool and stir into mayonnaise. Combine all remaining ingredients and blend this with the mayonnaise. Put into a lightly-oiled one quart mold. Chill and let congeal. Unmold by dipping into hot water for 5 seconds. Turn onto serving platter. Garnish with hard-cooked eggs, black olives and shrimp. Serve with saltine crackers.

CRABMEAT QUICHE

Line unbaked pie shell with:
½ lb. Swiss cheese cut in ¼" thick pieces.
Cover with layer of:
1 C crabmeat and ½ C small cooked shrimp

Combine:

1½ C light cream	½ t salt
4 eggs, beaten	dash pepper
1 T flour	dash cayenne
	¼ t nutmeg

Stir in:

2 T melted butter	2 T dry sherry

Beat well. Pour over seafood. Refrigerate or freeze. When ready to serve, bring to room temperature and bake at 375° for 40 minutes. Let stand for 20 minutes.

CRABMEAT ROUNDS

1 can of white crabmeat	1 C shredded cheddar cheese
Dash of mayonnaise	Melba toast rounds

Mix all ingredients together and spread on melba rounds. Place in oven and heat until cheese melts.

CURRIED CRAB CRESCENTS

1 Can (7½ oz.) crabmeat
1 Can water chestnuts,
   drained and sliced
½ C shredded Swiss cheese
1/3 C mayonnaise
2 T chopped onion

1 T lemon juice
1 T pimiento
1 t Worcestershire
¼ t salt
¼ t curry powder

Spread mixture on crescent rolls. Do opposite of directions on can. Bake in oven at 400° until brown.

GOURMET SHRIMP

2 lb. shrimp
4 t butter
¼ C parsley

1 clove garlic
¾ t salt

Saute raw peeled shrimp in all ingredients until pink. Serve on picks.

HOT MUSTARD SHRIMP

1/3 C red wine vinegar
1 t ketchup
¼ t horseradish
3 t hot mustard
1½ lbs. shelled deveined
   cooked shrimp

2 minced cloves garlic
¼ t salt
Dash pepper
1/3 C oil
Chives

In a large bowl, combine vinegar, ketchup, horseradish, mustard, garlic, salt and pepper. Blend in oil. Add shrimp. Chill. Serve in a bowl with toothpicks; garnish with chives. Serves 6.

LITTLE CLAMBAKES

1 pkg. (8 oz.) cream cheese	½ t liquid red-pepper seasoning
1 8 oz. can minced clams	4 doz. buttery crackers
1 T bottled onion juice	Paprika

Soften cheese in medium-sized bowl. Drain clams very well; add to cheese along with onion juice and red pepper seasoning. Mix well. (May store covered in refrigerator.) Just before serving, spread clam mixture on crackers (about 1 teaspoon on each) and sprinkle lightly with paprika. Place on large cookie sheet and bake in 400° oven for 5 minutes (until heated through but not brown). Garnish with sliced black olives and watercress leaves. Makes 4 dozen.

MARINATED SHRIMP

1 C vinegar	1 clove garlic
¼ C olive oil	½ C chili sauce
1 T hot mustard	⅛ t salt
½ C chopped onions	2 T paprika
	2 lbs. shrimp, boiled

Mix all ingredients and marinate shrimp. Serve in the sauce.

MUSHROOMS STUFFED WITH CRABMEAT

20 large mushrooms,
stemmed
½ t melted butter
6½ oz. crabmeat
1 egg
1 heaping T of mayonnaise

¼ t minced onion
1 T lemon juice
½ C bread crumbs
(Use ¼ C bread crumbs for
mushroom mixture and
drizzle ¼ C over
mushrooms)

Dip caps in melted butter. Place upside down in baking dish on foil.
Combine ingredients. Fill caps and sprinkle with crumbs and drizzle
with butter. Bake 15-25 minutes at 375°.

OYSTERS ANCHOVY

Cut 1½ lbs. good sharp American cheese into small pieces. In a skillet,
heat to the sizzling point, a piece of butter or margarine about the size
of an egg. Add three pounds of frozen or fresh oysters and let them
cook until their edges curl. Strain oysters and measure juice. Add to
juice enough milk to make 6 cups in all and heat this liquid.

In sauce pan, melt 5 T butter and blend in 6 T flour. Remove from
heat, add hot liquid slowly, stirring constantly.

Open 4 2-oz. cans fillets of anchovy. Leave anchovies in can, strain off
liquid and let some cold water wash them off. Strain gently, mash
fillets with fork and add them to the cheese and hot milk mixture.
Cook until the cheese is melted and sauce smooth and thick. Stir constantly or it will scorch.

Add oysters and cook a little. If they are going to give off more juice,
let it be now.

Blend 2 T cornstarch with ½ C cold milk and add a little at a time until sauce is thick enough to spoon onto a piece of melba toast. Add a
dash of Tabasco sauce (add more if needed). Can make ahead and
reheat.

OYSTERS ROCKEFELLER

12 baking shells
12 fresh oysters
¾ C sour cream
2 to 4 cloves finely
  chopped or pressed garlic
  (I use garlic powder)
Salt, pepper, dash cayenne

1 T butter
1 C raw finely chopped
  spinach
1 T bread crumbs and
  parmesan cheese
  (combined)
½ C whipped cream (touch
  white pepper)

Mix spinach with sour cream. Add garlic, salt, pepper and cayenne. Place a small amount of mixture in the baking shell and cover with one oyster. Sprinkle with bread crumbs and parmesan cheese combined. Dot with butter. Brown under the broiler. Remove and put one T whipped cream on top of each oyster. Brown under broiler again. Serve hot. Delicious!

OYSTERS WITH BACON

6 slices bacon
12 fresh oysters
1 t Worcestershire sauce

Salt and pepper to taste
1 T lemon juice

Preheat oven to 400°. Cut bacon strips in half and cook until partially done; drain. Season oysters and wrap each oyster in half a slice of bacon; secure with a toothpick. Bake at 400° on a rack over a shallow pan for 5 to 7 minutes or until bacon is done. Serve hot. Yield: 1 dozen.

PANACEA SHRIMP

Large shrimp
Bacon

Pancake mix (omit egg
and oil)
Milk (enough to make
loose batter)

Wrap large shrimp with ½ strip bacon. Secure with toothpick. Dip into a loose batter and fry. Serve hot.

PARTY SALAMI ROLLS

7-oz. can tuna
1 hard cooked egg,
chopped
¼ C mayonnaise

1 t lemon juice
Sliced party salami
Mozzarella cheese

Combine tuna, egg, mayonnaise and lemon juice. Roll up cheese and 1 t tuna in salami. Put in 3 toothpicks. Chill and slice.

SHERRIED CLAMS

2 small onions, diced
2 medium green peppers,
diced
2 T butter
2 7½-oz. cans minced
clams, drained

½ lb. mild cheese,
grated
½ C ketchup
2 T dry sherry
Dash cayenne pepper

Saute onion and green pepper in butter until lightly browned. Add remaining ingredients and simmer over medium heat until cheese melts completely. Serve in scalloped seashell. Garnish center with sprig of parsley and serve on crackers of varying shapes. Yield: 3 cups.

SHRIMP CANAPES

1 lb. fresh cooked shrimp, minced	½ t grated lemon rind
1 T minced onion	¼ t salt
1 t minced celery	4 or 5 drops Tabasco
1 t green pepper	¾ C mayonnaise
	2 t lemon juice

Mix all ingredients. Spread on 36 bread rounds, crackers, etc.

SHRIMP FANTASIA

1 lb. shelled shrimp (uncooked)	2 t honey
1 small garlic clove, crushed	½ t grated onion
½ C butter	1 T grated ginger or ¼ t ground ginger
4 T lemon juice	½ t ground mustard or 2 t prepared mustard
1 t salt	Dash black pepper
Few drops of hot pepper sauce	

Saute onion and garlic in butter for 2 minutes. Add other ingredients and heat. Then cook shrimp in the mixture. Serve warm in chafing dish or fondue pot.

SHRIMP INEZ

¼ C butter or margarine	1½ lbs. shelled and cleaned
1 clove garlic	medium raw shrimp
½ t salt	Dash pepper
1 t monosodium glutamate	1/3 C chopped parsley

About 15 minutes before serving, melt butter in a large skillet. Add garlic, salt and monosodium glutamate and saute until garlic is golden. Add shrimp and saute, stirring constantly until shrimp are pink. Then sprinkle with pepper, add parsley, and cook about a minute. Serve in chafing dish or casserole with candle warmer.

SHRIMP MARINADE

2 lbs. or more shrimp	2 T capers and juice
1 large white, onion,	1½ t salt
sliced and separated	1 t dried dill weed
1½ C Kraft vegetable oil	¼ t monosodium glutamate
¾ C vinegar	Optional: Celery seed and/
	or Tabasco sauce

Combine all ingredients except onions and shrimp. Shake well. Put layer of shrimp and onion alternately and pour marinade over. Let sit in refrigerator at least 24 hours.

SHRIMP MIAMI

2 lbs. shrimp, fresh or frozen ¼ C salad oil 2 t salt	½ t white pepper ¼ C extra dry vermouth 2 T lime or lemon juice

Clean, wash and peel shrimp, leaving the last section of the shell on. Preheat electric frying pan to 320°. Add oil, salt, pepper and shrimp. Cook for 8 to 10 minutes or until shrimp are tender, stirring frequently. Increase temperature to 420°. Add vermouth and lime juice. Cook one minute longer, stirring constantly. Drain. Serve hot or cold.

SHRIMP MOLD

1 8-oz. pkg. cream cheese
1 3-oz. pkg. cream cheese
3 T mayonnaise
½ envelope gelatin,
    softened in 2 T cold
    water and dissolved
    over hot water
Dash chili sauce
2 t Tabasco
	1 small onion, grated
	½ T lemon juice
	1 lb. cooked shrimp,
	    finely chopped
	½ C celery, finely chopped
	1 green pepper, finely
	    chopped
	2 hard-cooked eggs,
	    finely chopped
	Salt, pepper to taste

Whip together first 5 ingredients. Add other ingredients and pack into lightly oiled mold. Refrigerate until set. Unmold and serve with crackers. Serves 25.

SHRIMP ROUNDS

1 C mayonnaise	1 can shrimp, chopped
½ C finely grated American cheese	

Combine above ingredients. Cut bread into small rounds. Toast one side. Spread mixture on opposite side and then broil. Top with capers, parsley, etc., and serve hot.

SHRIMP STUFFED ARTICHOKES

1 jar cream cheese with chives	Tabasco, Worcestershire salt to taste
1 3-oz. pkg. cream cheese	2 cans artichoke hearts,
12 cooked, diced shrimp	not marinated
paprika	

Mash cheeses together. Add seasonings and shrimp. Mix well. Remove inside leaves of artichoke hearts and stuff with mixture. Sprinkle tops with paprika and broil until warm.

SMOKED OYSTERS

Roll thin 1 package pie crust mix and cut with small biscuit cutter. Place smoked oyster in center of dough round. Fold, press edges together and bake.

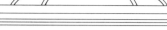

SHRIMP TOAST

Shrimp Mixture:

1 lb. raw shrimp, minced well or ground	1 t salt
2 heaping t ginger	few grains pepper
1 clove garlic, mashed	½ t Accent

Mix all ingredients well.

Batter:
4 egg whites
1 T cornstarch

Beat egg white and cornstarch and fold into shrimp mixture.

Meat mixture:

3 T ground meat	2 T onion, finely chopped
1 T wine	

Fold meat mixture into shrimp mixture and egg whites.

Bread:
1 loaf of day-old bread.

Cut crust off bread and cut slices into any desired shape. Shape small mounds of shrimp mixture onto bread slices. Heat oil for deep frying (oil 1" deep). Drop pieces into oil, shrimp side down. Fry until golden brown (6-8 minutes). Turn, quickly brown bottom and remove. Serve hot. Note: Mounded bread slices may be frozen before frying. Remove from freezer and thaw 1 hour before frying.

STUFFED COCKTAIL TOMATOES

1 Can crabmeat or tuna	1 t lemon juice
½ C finely diced celery	Salt and pepper to taste
¼ C grated onion	Mayonnaise
Cocktail tomatoes	

Mix seafood and other ingredients. Add enough mayonnaise to hold mixture together. Cut out inside of each tomato and fill with mixture.

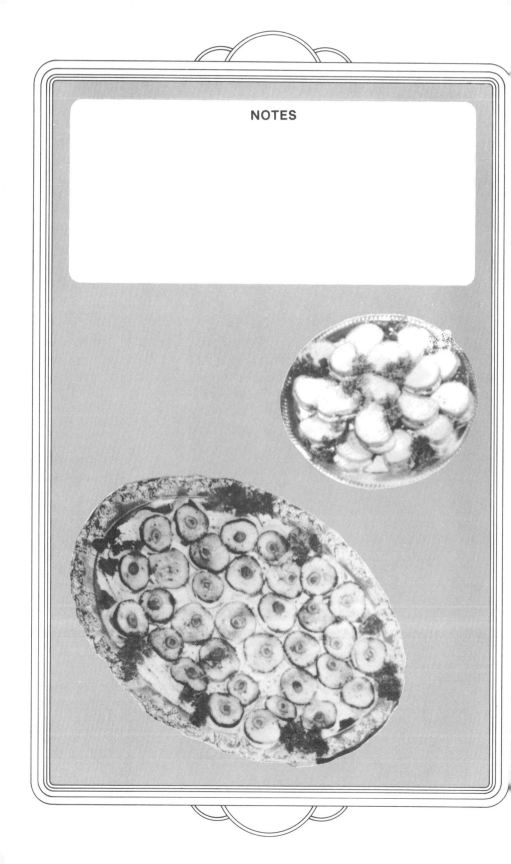

NOTES

BACON BISCUIT WITH DILL DIP

2 C biscuit mix	½ lb. bacon, fried and
2/3 C milk	crumbled
⅛ t pepper	1 egg, beaten
3 T green pepper	1 twin pkg. dill dip mix
1 T instant onion	1 C sour cream

Combine biscuit mix with milk, pepper, bacon, green pepper, onion. Roll out ½ inch thick. Cut with small biscuit cutter. Bake on ungreased cookie sheet at 450° for 8-10 min. Brush with beaten egg. Serve warm or cold with dip mixed with sour cream.

BACON NUTS

Bacon slices	Pecan halves

Cut each bacon strip in half. Wrap pecan half with bacon. Place fold side down on cookie sheet. Bake very slowly, watching carefully. Serve warm with tomato juice.

BLUE CHEESE BACON HORNS

1 pkg. 8-oz. cream cheese	3 T milk
1 pkg. 4-oz. blue cheese	1 T horseradish
6 slices crisp crumbled	1 t Worcestershire sauce
bacon	

Combine and dip or pipe into horn shaped corn snacks.

miscellaneous

BRANDIED GRAPES AND CHEESE

Seedless grapes   Gruyere Cheese
Brandy   Sugar

Skewer green seedless grapes on toothpicks. Dip in brandy and sprinkle with superfine sugar and let dry. Place a piece of Gruyere on each pick.

"CANAPE FLOWERPOTS"

Unsliced enriched bread   ¼ t salt
1 6½-oz. can crab   Dash of pepper
  meat flaked   1/3 C mayonnaise
1 C finely chopped celery   Sprigs of parsley
¼ C finely chopped
  green pepper
1 T lemon juice

Cut bread in 1 inch slices; freeze. Cut out circles from frozen slices with 1 inch round cutter. Hollow out centers with scissors, leaving bottom and sides about ¼ in. thick. Combine crab meat, celery, green pepper and seasonings. Add lemon juice and mayonnaise and mix well. Chill. Put filling in flowerpot. Garnish top with parsley.

CHEESE CRACKERS

1 stick butter   2 C nuts, chopped fine
1 lb. sharp cheese   3 C sifted flour

Let butter soften and grate cheese. Mix all four ingredients. Make rolls and slice ¼ inch thick. Bake at 350° for 15-20 min.

CHEESE CRESCENTS

3 oz. cream cheese
½ C shredded Cheddar
  mild
2 T green chilies
1 can crescent rolls

2 T ripe olives
1 T minced onion
5 drops Tabasco sauce

Mix all ingredients except rolls together. Piece 4 rolls together and make 2 squares. Spread with mixture. Bake at 375° for 12 min. Cut into 24 small pieces.

CHEESE SMOOTHIES

1 C butter
2 5-oz. jars sharp cheese spread
1½ C pancake mix
½ t caraway seed

Cream butter and cheese together. Add pancake mix and caraway seed. Blend well. Roll into small balls and place on greased baking sheet. Chill several hours. Bake at 375° for 10 min. and serve piping hot.

CHEESE STRAWS

2 sticks oleo
2 C plain flour
½ t salt

1 lb. sharp cheese,
  grated fine
1 t baking powder
¼ t red pepper

Beat butter and cheese with mixer till very smooth. Add other ingredients. Mash out of cookie press onto cookie sheet. Cook at 325°. Do not brown. Cool.

miscellaneous

CINDY'S CHUTNEY GOODIES

8-oz. pkg. cream cheese,
  softened
¼ C or less chutney

4 strips crisp bacon
Dash Tabasco

Crumble bacon into cheese. Mix in chutney and add Tabasco. Put on rounds of bread. Toast in oven for a very few seconds. These freeze very well. Take out of freezer, let thaw and then toast.

DUPREE'S FAVORITE SANDWICH LOAF

Ham salad with pickle
Chicken salad or tuna
Cream cheese with
  pineapple
Pimento cheese (sharp)

Egg salad with black
  olives
Peanut Butter
Jelly
Bakery bread

Have bakery slice loaf of bread in lengthwise slices. Trim away crusts. Stack the spreads from bottom layer up, beginning with ham salad. Always spread mayonnaise on bottom of top layer of bread. This will prevent the sandwich loaf from becoming dry. Make several days ahead, wrap in moistened towel. This will be a lovely ribbon sandwich when sliced. Also iced with whipped cream cheese and decorated with olives and pimentos, this becomes a colorful centerpiece. It is great for luncheons, served with potato chips and congealed salad.

FROZEN CHEESE CANAPE

½ lb. sharp
  Cheddar cheese
6 slices bacon,
  cooked not crisp
½ t Worcestershire

1 small onion
1 t dry mustard
2 t mayonnaise

Put cheese, bacon, and onion through food grinder. Add remaining ingredients. Mix well and form into roll about ½ inch in diameter. Wrap securely and freeze. Keep frozen til ready to use. Cut into ¼ inch slices, place on bread or cracker rounds. Place under broiler until golden brown.

GERMAN PANCAKES

4 eggs
1 T sugar
½ t salt

2/3 C sifted flour
2/3 C milk
2 T soft butter

Heat oven to 400°. Butter well 2 9" cake pans. Put eggs into blender container, cover and process at STIR until light yellow in color. Push MIX button, remove cover and add remaining ingredients; process until smooth. Pour into prepared pans and bake for 20 min., then reduce heat to 350° and bake 10 min. Slide onto hot plates. Serve with lemon slices, powdered sugar and butter. Syrup, jelly, honey or flavored butter may also be served. Serves four.

GOLDEN HORS D'OEUVRES

1 pkg. 4-oz. Blue Cheese, crumbled
1 pkg. 8-oz. cream cheese, softened
¾ t dry mustard
1 1/3 C moist toasted coconut

Cream together Blue Cheese and cream cheese until soft. Add mustard and mix well. Shape into small balls about ½ inch in diameter. Roll in coconut. Makes about 40 small balls.

ICE BOX CHEESE WAFERS

½ lb. grated sharp cheese
¼ lb. butter, creamed
1½ C sifted plain flour

Heavy pinch cayenne pepper
½ t salt
½ C finely chopped pecans

Cream together cheese, butter, salt and pepper. Add flour. Add nuts. Make into a roll. Wrap in waxed paper and put in ice box. Will keep a month. Slice into thin wafers and bake at 350° until golden brown. Makes 6-8 dozen.

MAPLY APPETIZERS

1 13½ - oz. can
  pineapple chunks
2 8 - oz. pkg. brown-
  and-serve sausage
  links
½ C maple-flavored syrup
1 green pepper cut in
  ¾ in. squares
½ C drained maraschino
  cherries

4 t cornstarch
½ t salt
1/3 C water
1/3 C vinegar

Drain pineapple, saving syrup. Cut sausages in thirds crosswise. Brown in skillet. Combine cornstarch, salt, pineapple syrup, maple syrup, water and vinegar. Heat until boils, stirring constantly. Add pineapple, sausage, pepper, and cherries. Cook five minutes. Keep warm in chafing dish, serving with cocktail picks.

MINIATURE CREAM PUFFS

1 C boiling water
½ C butter

1 C all-purpose flour
4 eggs

Pour water into a saucepan, add butter and bring to a boil. Reduce heat, add flour all at once stirring rapidly. Cook and stir until mixture thickens and leaves sides of pan - about 2 minutes. Remove from heat - add eggs one at a time beating thoroughly after each addition. Then beat until mixture looks satiny and breaks off when spoon is raised. Drop by teaspoonfuls about 1 inch apart on ungreased baking sheets. Bake at 425° for 30 minutes or until done. Cool. Yield 4 to 6 dozen small cream puffs.

FILLINGS FOR CREAM PUFFS
DEVILED CHEESE FILLING

1 C shredded
  American cheese
¼ t dry mustard
½ t Worcestershire
  sauce
3 T mayonnaise

1 t grated onion
5 drops Tabasco
¼ t celery seed

Mix all ingredients together. Split cream puff and fill. Yield 1 cup filling.

SHRIMP AND CHEESE FILLING

½ C flaked cooked
  shrimp
1 T freshly squeezed
  lemon juice
¼ C shredded sharp
  Cheddar cheese
Salt and pepper to
  taste

1 T chopped pimento
3 T mayonnaise
Paprika

Mix all ingredients, split cream puff and fill. Garnish with paprika. Yield 1 cup.

MUSHROOM ROLLS

1 loaf king size
  sandwich bread
1 can cream of
  mushroom soup
1½ t Worcestershire

2 T grated onion
½ to 1 stick of
  butter

Cut crust from bread. Roll each piece out until paper thin. Blend ingredients except butter and spread on each slice. Roll like jelly roll and place on cookie sheet with rolled side down. Brush with melted butter and broil in oven.

NACHOS

1 can refried beans
Grated sharp Cheddar
  cheese

1 bag of Doritos
1 small can Jalapeno
  pepper

Place small amount of refried beans on Doritos. Sprinkle with grated cheese. Top with small piece of Jalapeno pepper. Bake at 350° for 10-15 minutes until cheese melts.

OLIVE HORS D'OEUVRES

Cream cheese
Salt
Pepper

Green olives
Onion salt
Finely chopped chipped
  beef

Thin cream cheese with cream until it forms heavy paste. Season to taste with seasonings. Roll this mixture around small stuffed olive until you have a ball one inch across. Roll balls in chipped beef. Chill. Cut in half to serve. Serve cut side up.

OLIVE QUICHE

1 C slivered ripe
  olives
1 pint sour cream
1 t oregano
1½ C shredded
  Swiss cheese
6 eggs

2 T chives
¾ t salt
Dash cayenne pepper
Pastry for double
  pie crust

Beat eggs with wooden spoon. Add all ingredients and mix well. Prepare pastry according to instructions, roll out to fit a 15 x 10 x 1 inch jellyroll pan, bringing pastry partially upsides of pan. Pour olive mixture over pastry and bake 425° for 15 min. Reduce temperature to 375° and bake for 25 minutes or until filling is set. Cool slightly. Cut and serve warm. Serves 48 bars.

PARTY MIX RECIPE

6 T butter	2 C Corn Chex
4 t Worcestershire	2 C Rice Chex
1 t seasoned salt	2 C pretzels
2 C Wheat Chex	¾ C salted nuts

Heat oven to 250°. Melt butter in a shallow pan over low heat. Stir in Worcestershire and seasoned salt. Add assorted cereals and nuts. Mix over low heat until all pieces are coated. Heat 45 minutes in the oven, stirring every 15 minutes. Spread out on absorbent paper to cool. Yields 6¾ cups.

PARTY SANDWICH

Small dill pickles	Loaf thin bread
8-oz. cream cheese	

Trim slice of bread and press with a rolling pin till real thin. Spread with softened cream cheese. Roll around dill pickles. Chill and then slice in thin rounds.

PEPPERY SPICED NUTS

2 T butter, melted	Dash hot pepper sauce
1 lb. pecan or	½ t salt
walnut halves	⅛ t pepper
2 t Worcestershire	

Preheat oven to 325°. In skillet saute pecans in butter until hot. Add remaining ingredients. Arrange nuts in shallow pan and bake at 325° for 20 minutes. Yield: 4 cups.

PIZZA POPCORN

1/3 C butter
1 small clove
  garlic, minced
½ to 1 t oregano

8 cups cooked popcorn
2 T grated
  Parmesan cheese

In saucepan, melt butter with garlic and oregano. Pour over popcorn and mix well. Toss with cheese. Makes 8 cups.

PUFFS

½ C water
¼ C butter
¼ t salt

½ C sifted all-purpose
  flour
2 eggs

Bring water to boil in saucepan on high. Add butter and stir until melted. Switch to low, add flour and salt. Stirring vigorously. Cook until mixture draws away from the sides of the pan. Remove and cool one minute. Add eggs, one at a time, beating after each addition until smooth. On greased baking pan, drop batter by teaspoons 2 inches apart. Bake in a 400° oven for 40 minutes. When cool fill puffs with favorite shrimp, crab, etc.

QUICHE

Cheddar cheese
Monterey Jack cheese

2 eggs
Green chilies

Layer Cheddar, then green chilies, then Cheddar, then green chilies and then Monterey Jack cheese. Beat eggs and pour over the entire dish. Use flat pyrex dish. Bake 20 minutes at 400°. This must be sliced into squares and served on small plates with fork.

QUICHE INDIVIDUALS

2 small pkg. cream
   cheese
2 sticks butter

2 C flour

Mix well and chill. Divide and shape into tiny muffin pans.

6 oz. grated Swiss
   cheese
1 bottle Bacos
3 eggs
2 C ½ & ½ cream

½ t dry mustard
1 t Worcestershire
1 t salt

Put Bacos on bottom of each tart, then put a good pinch of cheese. Put all other ingredients into blender. Mix for a few seconds and pour over cheese and Bacos in pies. Bake at 350-375° for 30 min., or until nicely browned on top. Freezes well and may be warmed in slow 200° oven on biscuit tray. Makes 48.

QUICHE LORRAINE

1 t chopped onion
6 slices bacon
6 oz. sliced Swiss
   cheese
2 C milk

4 eggs
½ t salt
Dash pepper
Dash cayenne

Fry or broil bacon. Heat the milk slowly. Line 9" pie plate with plain pastry. Place chopped onion and bacon on pastry and cover with cheese slices. Beat the eggs and gradually add the hot milk and then the salt, pepper, and cayenne. Pour mixture into pastry. Bake in 450° oven for 10 minutes. Reduce to 300° and bake until custard is firm. Let cool slightly before serving. Cut in small wedges to serve as hors d'oeuvres.

ROQUEFORT BISCUITS

¼ lb. Roquefort
 or blue cheese
¼ lb. softened butter
1 1/3 C sifted all-
 purpose flour

2 T whipping cream
1 egg yolk

Mash cheese in a bowl with mixing fork. Beat in butter, cream and egg yolk, then knead in flour. Shape into a ball and wrap with waxed paper. Chill until firm. Roll out ¼ inch thick and cut into 1½ inch rounds. Brush with egg and bake at 425° 10 to 15 minutes. These may be baked, frozen and reheated for 5 minutes. Makes 3 dozen.

RYE BREAD AND CHEESE

loaf rye bread
 (round)
1 jar Cheese Whiz

Beer

Scoop out center of round loaf of rye bread. Melt Cheese Whiz with beer to moisten. Put in rye bread and dip hunks of rye into it. May substitute dark pumpernickle and may add crab.

SOUR CREAM ROLLS

1 can Crescent rolls
1 C sour cream
1 T Parmesan cheese

Garlic salt
2 T chopped onion
3 slices crumbled
 cooked bacon

Mix all ingredients except rolls together. Divide rolls into four rectangular sections. Spread mixture on rolls. Roll up sections and slice into circles, baking at 375° til browned. Bake 10 to 12 minutes.

miscellaneous

STUFFED BLACK OLIVES

3 T butter
1 t minced parsley
1 green onion,
   chopped
½ t vinegar
2 t anchovy paste

1 t minced capers
2 t minced sweet
   pickles
½ t salt
¼ t paprika
40 large, pitted
   black olives

Cream all ingredients together except olives. Then fill olives with mixture.

STUFFED DILL PICKLES

1 small jar Old English Cheese spread
2 dill pickles

Slice end off pickles. Carefully remove center with apple corer. Remove all possible moisture; drain. Fill center with cheese, pack firmly. Wrap tightly with waxed paper; refrigerate for several hours or longer. Slice just before serving. If served on round crackers, cut thinner slices.

STUFFED EGGS

12 hard cooked
   eggs, halfed
1 C (8-oz.) cooked
   crab meat, flaked
1 C finely chopped
   celery
1 T French salad
   dressing

2 T finely chopped
   green pepper
1/3 C sour cream

Mix all well, stuff egg halves and chill.

TOASTED CHEESE ROLLS

1 loaf whole wheat
  bread, sliced thin
1 jar sharp
  processed cheese

Butter

Trim crusts from bread and roll each slice very thin with a rolling pin. Spread with a thin layer of cheese and roll very tight. Cut each roll in two pieces. and fasten each with a toothpick. Place on baking sheet. These should be brushed with melted butter and baked till toasty at 375°.

WATERMELON COOLER

Watermelon
Cantaloupe

Honeydew
Strawberries

Prepare melon balls from watermelon, cantaloupe, and honeydew. Chill thoroughly. Right before serving time pour melon balls into scooped out watermelon half. Garnish with fresh strawberries. Provide toothpicks for spearing melon balls.

CUCUMBER ROUNDS

2 long cucumbers

Soak in ice water 2 hours. Drain on paper towel. Score with fork. Slice in thin slices (25 to 30 slices per cucumber).

Loaf of white bread
1 C mayonnaise
6 T sour cream
3 T grated onion
dash garlic powder

Remove crust from bread. Cut into rounds with small biscuit cutter. Spread with dressing and top with sliced cucumber. Sprinkle with paprika. Top with sliced stuffed olive.

CRUMBLY CHEESE COOKIES

2 sticks soft oleo   **2 C Rice Krispies**
1 C flour   **Red pepper**
2 C grated sharp
** Cheddar cheese**

Mix and form balls; flatten slightly with fork. Bake at 375° for 10-12 minutes. Makes 50 small "cookies."

NOTES

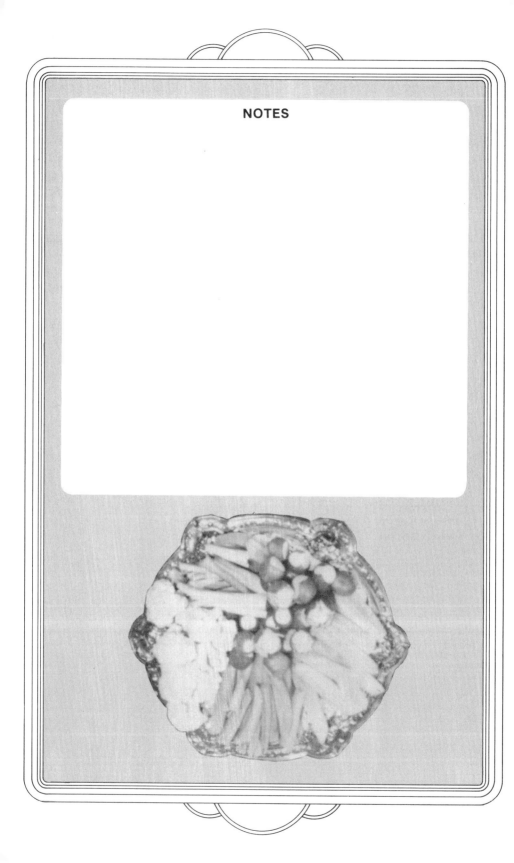

ANTIPASTA

2 2½-oz. cans whole mushrooms (drained)
2 14-oz. cans artichoke hearts (Rinse with
  water and drain)
2 16-oz. cans whole Blue Lake green
  beans (drained)
1 can pitted black olives (drained)
1 7-oz. bottle salad olives (drained)
1 bottle Italian Giardiniera (do not drain)
1 or 2 onions (sliced and divided into rings)
1 green pepper (cut into strips and add just
  before serving)

Put all ingredients (except green pepper) into large bowl, keeping as separated as possible. Pour over them marinade made of:

1 t minced onion	Dash garlic salt
Dash lemon pepper	1 t sugar
Dash black pepper	2 cloves garlic (pressed)
2 t salt	½ C olive or salad oil
	¾ C wine vinegar

Cover and refrigerate. Make day before serving and stir marinade around vegetables several times during day. Drain vegetables before serving on large platter. Must be served with small plates and forks. Not finger foods!

APPETIZER MUFFINS

2 T shredded carrot	2 C packaged biscuit mix
2 T finely chopped celery	1 T sugar
2 T finely chopped onion	½ C shredded cheddar
1 T butter	cheese
1 4½-oz. can	1 egg
deviled ham	2/3 C milk

In small skillet, cook until tender, carrots, celery and onion in butter. Cool. Stir in deviled ham. In medium bowl combine remaining ingredients; beat by hand ½ minute. Fill one ¾" greased muffin pan 2/3 full of batter. Make an indention in center of each and fill with a little ham mixture. Bake in 400° oven about 15 minutes until browned. Remove from pans while hot; cool on rack.

ARTICHOKE BALLS

2 14-oz. cans artichoke	2 eggs, beaten
hearts	2 T lemon juice
1 box seasoned bread	3 cloves of garlic,
crumbs	pressed
2 T salad oil	
Grated Romano cheese	

Drain and chop artichoke hearts; add bread crumbs, eggs, oil, lemon juice and garlic. Mix well; form into bite-sized balls. Roll in cheese; serve with wooden picks.

ARTICHOKE HEARTS IN ROQUEFORT SAUCE

2 cans small artichoke
  hearts (cut heart in half)
1 large pkg. of Roquefort
  cheese (not Bleu Cheese)
2 sticks butter

1 T parsley flakes
¼ t Tabasco
1 t Worcestershire
  juice of 2 lemons

Melt butter and cheese over low heat and add seasonings - then artichoke hearts. Heat thoroughly. Serve with crackers or Melba toast.

ASPARAGUS ROLL-UPS

1 large can asparagus
  spears
1 3-oz. pkg. cream cheese

Dash onion salt
Bread (with crusts removed)

Drain asparagus spears. Soften cream cheese and mix with onion salt to taste. Spread cheese on slice of bread and roll around asparagus spear. Secure with toothpick. Serve.

vegetables

CHERRY TOMATOES

½ C finely chopped
  cooked ham
¼ C or 1-oz. Roquefort
  cheese (crumbled)
½ C sour cream

¼ t lemon juice
Dash pepper
36 cherry tomatoes
parsley flakes

Combine first 5 ingredients in small bowl. Refrigerate until ready to use. Cut tops from tomatoes and scoop out insides. Put ½ t of mixture in each tomato and garnish with parsley.

CELERY RINGS

3 T butter
1 3-oz. pkg. cream cheese
3 T tomato paste

Salt
Red pepper
1 stalk celery

Cream butter; add cheese and tomato paste. Season to taste with salt and red pepper. Stuff all pieces of celery with mixture. First put hearts together, then place other pieces of celery around and make the stalk its original shape. Wrap in waxed paper and chill. Slice; make rings and serve.

CHEESE STUFFED LETTUCE

1 medium head lettuce
1 3-oz. pkg. cream cheese
¾ C cottage cheese
½ C raw carrots,
  grated

⅛ t pepper
3 T chopped green pepper
¼ C nuts
¼ t salt
½ T minced onion

Core lettuce, making cavity large enough for ingredients. Blend remaining ingredients and pack into cavity. Chill 2-3 hours. Cut into wedges. May be served with French dressing. Yield: 6-8 Servings.

CUCUMBER SPEARS WITH CRAB DIP

1 medium green pepper
1 C sour cream
1 can 7½-oz. crabmeat,
   drained and cartilage
   removed

½ t garlic salt
¼ t grated lemon peel
1 large cucumber

Cut thin slice from stem end of green pepper. Remove seeds and membranes. Place sour cream, crabmeat, garlic salt and lemon peel in blender. Blend on medium-high speed until smooth (45 seconds). Pour into green pepper shell. Pare cucumber; slice. Makes 4 servings.

CUCUMBERS STUFFED WITH SPINACH

3 cucumbers
1 10-oz. pkg. frozen
   chopped spinach
2 T Durkee's dressing

Pepper to taste
Pimiento strips

Peel cucumbers and cut into one-inch thick pieces. With a small melon ball scooper, scoop out seeds from cucumbers pieces, leaving a bottom ¼-inch thick. After cooking spinach as directed, drain and combine with dressing and pepper. Fill each cucumber center with the spinach mixture, topping with a pimiento strip. Chill.

DELICIOUS CUCUMBERS

2 or 3 cucumbers (peel and
   slice thin)

Cover with salt water for about one hour. Rinse well and dry. Mix ¼ C vinegar and 2 heaping tablespoons mayonnaise and pour over cucumbers. Cover and refrigerate until ready to serve.

vegetables

FRENCH FRIED MUSHROOMS

1 egg	1/3 C flour
½ C milk	1 C cornflake crumbs
½ t salt	fresh mushrooms

Beat egg, milk and salt. Roll mushrooms in flour, then dip in egg mixture. Roll in crumbs to coat completely. In electric skillet or heavy saucepan, heat salad oil (1½ to 2" deep) to 375°. Drop mushrooms in gently, fry until golden brown, about 1 minute on each side. Drain on paper towels. Sprinkle with salt. Serve with lemon wedges.

FRIED CHILI PEPPERS

1 can Jalapeno green chili peppers	cornmeal
Mozzarella or Muenster cheese	salt
1 egg	

Drain peppers. Slice open peppers and remove seeds. Place 3 or 4 strips of Mozzarella or Muenster cheese in center. Close with toothpicks and dip in egg (beaten) then into meal (lightly salted). Fry and serve hot.

HOT ONION CANAPES

Sliced white bread	Onion, thinly sliced
Mayonnaise or salad dressing	Parmesan cheese

Cut circles of bread about 1½" in diameter. Spread mayonnaise on each bread round. Put thin slice of onion on this. Sprinkle with Parmesan cheese. You may bake in preheated oven (400°) or broil until cheese is lightly toasted.

MARINATED ARTICHOKE HEARTS

Slice canned artichoke hearts in half lengthwise. Place in large jar or bowl and cover with bottled Italian dressing (or your own). Let marinate at least 24 hours in refrigerator. When ready to serve, drain and place in crystal bowl. Scatter stuffed and ripe olives over top. Serve with toothpicks.

MARINATED MUSHROOMS

120 fresh button mushrooms	2½ C olive oil
20 lemons (5 Cups lemon juice)	Salt and pepper

Wash and peel mushrooms. Place 24 mushrooms per shallow dish and pour juice of 4 lemons and ½ C olive oil over them. Marinate for at least 2 hours. Drain and serve with individual cocktail picks.

MARINATED MUSHROOMS

1 lb. mushrooms	1 t Accent
5-oz. wine vinegar	3 lemons (juice)
3-oz. Wesson Oil	1-oz. sugar
½ t oregano	¼ t mustard powder
½ t salt	
½ Bermuda onion, diced	

Wash mushrooms very well in cold water. Add all ingredients and mix well. Cover the bowl with cheese cloth, place in refrigerator and let the mushrooms marinate for two days.

MARINATED VEGETABLE TRAY

Marinate fresh mushrooms and squash overnight in Italian dressing. Marinate cauliflower and carrots for an hour before serving in Catalina dressing. Serve with cocktail picks.

MINIATURE ASPIC ROUNDS

2 jars (48) small artichoke hearts or
48 small cheese balls (Bleu, Cheddar, or a mixture of cream
cheese seasoned to taste)
3 C favorite tomato aspic recipe
48 melba toast rounds

Grease smallest size muffin tins with oil. Place artichoke hearts or cheese balls in each cup. Spoon in a small amount of slightly thickened aspic. Chill until set. Invert molds on toast rounds.

MUSHROOM TURNOVERS

Pastry:
3 3-oz. pkgs. cream cheese at room temperature
1½ C flour
½ C butter at room temperature

Mix cheese and butter then add flour til smooth. Chill!!

Filling:

3 T butter	**freshly-ground pepper to**
1 large onion, chopped	**taste**
½ lb. mushrooms,	**2 T flour**
finely chopped	**¼ C sour cream**
¼ t thyme	**¼ C white wine**
1½ t salt	

Heat butter and add mushrooms and onions. Saute until soft (about 3 minutes). Add thyme, salt, pepper and flour. Stir in sour cream. Cook until thick. Add wine. Roll out dough ⅛" thick. Cut with 3" biscuit cutter. Fill with 1 teaspoon filling. Fold over and prick. Bake at 450° for 15 minutes on an ungreased cookie sheet. Makes 2 dozen.

PARTY ONION SANDWICHES

Cut thin slices of onions. Cut bread rounds approximately the same size as onions. Place onion on bread and put spoonful of mayonnaise on top. Sprinkle with paprika and parmesan cheese. Put under broiler until top is slightly brown. Serve hot.

PICKLED SQUASH

1 lb. squash	2 to 3 pods garlic, crushed
1 C Mazola Oil	1 t to 1 T Worcestershire
1/3 to ¼ C vinegar	Sauce
1 t salt	Optional: 2 to 3 green hot
	peppers (crushed) cracked
	black pepper

Slice squash (cross section). Do not peel. Marinate 2 or 3 days at room temperature. Then refrigerate and serve with toothpicks.

SAUTEED CHERRY TOMATOES

Cherry tomatoes	Salt
¼ C butter (per small	
basket of cherry tomatoes)	

Rinse a small basket of cherry tomatoes. Drain well and remove stems. Saute tomatoes in skillet with butter. Shake (Do not stir) skillet vigorously until the tomato skins are slightly wrinkled. Season to taste and serve.

SAUTEED MUSHROOMS

Crush 8 to 10 cloves of garlic and saute in one stick of butter until soft. Add mushrooms (1 lb.) and cook over low heat until the liquid evaporates and only butter and mushrooms are left.

STUFFED BEETS

Scoop out centers of tiny rosebud beets; fill with highly seasoned diced hard-boiled eggs mixed with a cooked dressing or softened cream cheese. Put cocktail picks in sides of beets.

STUFFED MUSHROOMS

**1 lb. medium-size
  mushrooms
½ lb. bacon**

1 lb. sharp cheddar cheese

Wash mushrooms. Cut off mushroom stems and dice. Saute caps in butter. Fry bacon until crisp, then crumble. Pour off some bacon drippings then saute stems in grease and drain. Add stems to cheese and bacon while hot. Mix all ingredients and stuff into caps. Broil until cheese becomes bubbly.

NOTES

AVOCADO DIP OR DRESSING

1 ripe avocado
¼ C salad oil
¼ C vinegar

¼ C sour cream
½ C blue cheese

Mash avocado in mixer or blender. Add oil and vinegar alternately. Add sour cream and crumbled blue cheese. Mix till fairly smooth. Chill before serving.

BLACK BEAN DIP

Gradually blend 1 can condensed black bean soup (Campbell's) into one three ounce package of softened cream cheese. Add 1/3 cup chopped fresh tomatoes, 3 tablespoons minced onion, and 3 tablespoons chili powder. Chill and serve with corn chips.

BLUE CHEESE DUNK

Combine one cup crumbled blue cheese (4 ounces), one 3 ounce package of cream cheese (softened), 2 tablespoons milk, and 2 tablespoons salad dressing. Beat with electric mixer till fluffy or use electric blender. Serve with celery, carrots, or cauliflower dippers.

CAULIFLOWER DIP

1 block cream cheese
2 T mayonnaise
2 t prepared mustard
1 T chives

1 head cauliflower
lemon juice to taste
salt, pepper, paprika
    to taste

Mix ingredients and dip cauliflower.

CAVIAR DIP WITH SOUR CREAM

½ pint sour cream
1 small jar caviar
½ t lemon juice

Dash Worcestershire sauce
Dash Tabasco

Mix all together well. Serve with rye bread or crackers.

CHEDDAR CHEESE FONDUE

½ C Sauterne or other dry white wine
1 medium clove minced garlic
4 ounces natural Swiss cheese cut in pieces
2 T flour
1 can (10¾ ounces) condensed cheddar cheese soup
French or Italian bread cubes

In saucepan or fondue pot simmer wine and garlic. Combine cheese and flour. Gradually stir into wine. Heat until cheese melts, stirring now and then. Blend in soup, heat, stirring until smooth. Makes 2 cups.

CHILI CON QUESO DIP

2 T Wesson oil
2 onions, chopped fine
1 jalapeno pepper,
  chopped
1 can tomatoes,
  drained
2 cloves garlic

2 lb. Velveeta cheese
½ T black pepper
1 T salt
1 4-oz. jar pimento,
  drained, chopped

Brown onions in oil. Add all ingredients in a double boiler except cheese. Simmer 10 minutes. Add small pieces of cheese until all is melted. Keep warm while serving. Best when served with Fritos. Can be frozen.

CLAM DIGGER'S DUNK

1 can (10 ounce) condensed New England clam chowder
  soup
1 large package cream cheese, softened
1 can (4 ounces) mushrooms, drained and chopped
1 T finely chopped onion
Dash cayenne pepper

With mixer gradually blend soup into cream cheese on slow speed. Add remaining ingredients. Chill and serve with crackers or chips. Makes 2½ cups.

CLAM DIP

1 C sour cream   Garlic powder
2 cans drained clams   lemon juice
Parsley   Salt to taste

Blend ingredients and serve with crackers or chips.

CLAM DIP

2 8-ounce packages cream cheese
½ carton sour cream (8-ounce size)
1 can Snow's minced clams
4 dashes Worcestershire sauce

Drain clams, reserving juice. Combine above ingredients. Add small amount of juice until it is the desired consistency.

CUCUMBER CHEESE DIP

1 large cucumber	2 T lemon juice
2 3-ounce packages	2 T chopped onion
cream cheese	

Coarsely grate peeled cucumber, drain, reserving liquid. Stir and soften cream cheese, add lemon juice. Stir in onion and cucumber. Milk may be added to reach desired consistency.

CURRY DIP

1 C mayonnaise	1 t prepared horseradish
1 t curry powder	1 t vinegar
1 t grated onion	dash garlic powder

Mix well. Excellent for cauliflower, carrots, celery, or other raw vegetables. Makes one cup.

CURRY SAUCE FOR RAW VEGETABLES

½ C mayonnaise	2 T minced fresh parsley
1 C sour cream	½ t dried tarragon,
2 T fresh lemon juice	crushed
Salt and pepper	2 T grated onion
to taste	2 T prepared mustard
1 t curry powder	1 T minced chives
½ t paprika	several dashes Tabasco
1 T dill weed	

Combine all ingredients. Chill overnight. Use as dip for cauliflower, cucumbers, squash, celery or carrots.

EGGPLANT CAVIAR

3 medium eggplant
3 medium tomatoes, seeded
¼ C olive oil
1 medium onion, chopped
Seasonings: salt, pepper, dill weed, parsley, catsup to taste.

Boil eggplant until tender, cool, skin, deseed, chop into small pieces. Brown onion in olive oil, add seasonings, eggplant and tomatoes (cut up). Simmer for an hour, stirring occasionally or place in a casserole and bake for an hour. Serve hot with cheese on top or cold on dark rye bread.

FONDUE BEEF DIP

½ C mayonnaise
3 T horseradish
½ C chili sauce

Mix all ingredients together until well blended. Use as dip for beef chunks.

GUACAMOLE

2 ripe avocados   1 t salt
Juice of 1 lemon   1 t grated onion
1 medium clove
   garlic

Mash avocados and mix with other ingredients. Stick toothpick in clove of garlic. Remove before serving.

HEARTY CHEESE FONDUE

1¾ C milk
2 8-ounce packages cream cheese
2 t dry mustard
¼ C chopped green onions
(2¼ ounce) jar sliced dried beef, diced
French bread, cut in bite size pieces

Heat milk, add cream cheese. Stir until cream cheese is melted. Add mustard, onions and dried beef. Cook 5 minutes longer on low heat. Serve in chafing dish or fondue pot. Makes 10-12 servings.

HORSERADISH DIP

1 8-ounce package cream cheese	Salt
1 T mayonnaise	Lemon juice
6 slices cooked bacon (crisp)	2 t horseradish
Dash red pepper	

Blend ingredients together and serve with potato chips or Fritos.

HOT CHEESE 'N CRAB DIP

1 (6½ or 7½ ounce) can crab meat
1 (10 ounce) stick sharp cheddar cheese
1 (8 ounce) package sharp processed cheese, sliced
½ stick butter
½ C Sauterne

Shred crab meat, saving a few pieces for garnish. Cut cheese in small pieces. Combine in saucepan with the butter and Sauterne. Stir over low heat until cheese melts. Stir in crab meat and continue cooking till thoroughly heated. Pour into chafing dish and garnish with remaining crab pieces. Serve with Triscuits or chunks of crusty bread and fondue forks. Makes 3 cups.

HOT CRAB DIP

1 lb. Velveeta cheese (Cheddar cheese can be used)
1 can crab meat (6½ ounce)
2 T grated onion
Dash Worcestershire sauce
Milk or cream to thin as needed
1 tomato, chopped

Melt cheese, add remaining ingredients. Serve from chafing dish with crackers or chips.

HOT CRAB DIP

1 8-ounce package cream cheese 1 can crab meat 2 T sherry	Dash Tabasco 1/3 C almonds 1 t lemon juice

Combine all ingredients except almonds. Blend well and spoon into baking dish. Sprinkle with sliced almonds. Bake at 350° for 15-20 minutes. Serve with crackers.

HOT SEAFOOD DIP

½ lb. butter
1 C flour
1 small can
  evaporated milk
2 C milk
1 t paprika
1 t black pepper
	1 can mushrooms, cut
	  up fine
	2 cans crab meat
	1 lb. cooked shrimp
	Salt to taste
	1 bunch of onions,
	  cut up fine
	1½ C parsley, cut
	  up fine (optional)

Melt butter in top of double boiler. Slowly add flour, then milk and cream, making a white sauce. Add other ingredients and serve in chafing dish with Melba rounds.

HOT SHRIMP DIP

2 cans frozen shrimp
   soup
Garlic salt to taste
Pepper to taste
1 lb. Velveeta cheese

½ C milk
1 small can tomato paste
Lawry's seasoning
2 lbs. shrimp,
   cooked

Slowly heat soup, milk, tomato paste, and seasonings until soup has completely melted. Add cheese and shrimp. Serve hot from a chafing dish with corn chips.

PEAR DIP

4 fresh Bartlett pears
¼ t salt
½ t Worcestershire

1 small package cream
   cheese
1 (2½ ounce) jar Parmesan
   cheese
Mayonnaise to soften

Wash pears and chill. Combine remaining ingredients and beat until well mixed and creamy. Place in small bowl and sprinkle with paprika. Cut pears into quarters, then into eighths. Arrange on tray around cheese dip. Serve with crackers.

PICKLED SHRIMP DIP

½ lb. melted butter
2 T Worcestershire
pinch salt

3 T soy sauce
11 shots Tabasco sauce
Juice of 5 lemons

Melt butter and add other ingredients. Heat but do not boil.

QUICK TUNA DIP

¼ T Tabasco
3 T mayonnaise
1 T lemon juice

2 3-ounce package
   cream cheese
1 7-ounce can flaked
   tuna, drained
½ t grated onion

Blend Tabasco, cream cheese, and mayonnaise. Stir in tuna, lemon juice, and onion. Mix well. Makes 1½ cups.

RAW VEGETABLE DIP

1 can tomato soup
2 or 3 cloves garlic,
   cut
2 t dry mustard
½ C sugar
4 t grated onion

3 t salt
1 C oil
½ C vinegar
3 t Worcestershire sauce

Combine, adding vinegar and oil last. Can be used for shrimp also.

RED KIDNEY BEAN DIP

1 onion, chopped
  finely
2 cans red kidney
  beans
3 fresh tomatoes, cut
  in small chunks

½ to ¾ C olive oil
1½ Jalepeno peppers,
  chopped finely

Drain half the liquid from beans. With a fork, mash the beans in the remaining liquid or run the beans through a food chopper. In a heavy skillet such as cast iron, pour in olive oil, add remaining ingredients except tomatoes and onions. Simmer over low heat, stirring frequently and adding more oil to keep moist. The longer simmered the better - at least one hour. Just before serving, add fresh chopped tomato and onion.

SEAFOOD DIP

8 ounces cream cheese
2 T mayonnaise
1 T chopped onion
1 T parsley, dried
1 t Worcestershire

½ t prepared mustard
lemon juice
Salt
Milk
1 small can crab, clam, tuna,
  shrimp or other seafood

Combine cream cheese, mayonnaise, onion, parsley, Worcestershire, and mustard. Drain seafood and squeeze lemon juice over it. Add this to cream cheese mixture. Add salt to taste and soften to desired consistency with milk. Chill.

SHRIMP DIP

8 ounces cream cheese
¼ t onion juice
dash Worcestershire
paprika

1/3 C sour cream
2 t freshly squeezed
  lemon juice
1 C chopped cooked shrimp

Soften cheese and blend in sour cream and seasonings. Stir in shrimp and add paprika.

SHRIMP DIP

2 cans shrimp or
  crab
1 onion grated
1 C mayonnaise

1 small package Sharp
  Cracker Barrel Cheese,
  grated
dash of garlic salt

Mix all ingredients and serve. Use Fritos for dipping. This is better if made a day ahead.

SLIM-SATIONAL DIP

1 8-ounce bottle Low Calorie Blue Cheese or Thousand
  Island Dressing
1 C cottage cheese, sieved
2 T green onion slices

Combine ingredients. Mix well and chill. Serve with crisp vegetable dippers. Makes two cups.

SPINACH DIP

2 C mayonnaise
½ C green onions, chopped
A little parsley
1 package frozen spinach, thawed and squeezed dry

Mix and let set 24 hours before serving.

STEVE'S COCKTAIL SAUCE

½ C horseradish
1 C chili sauce
Juice of 2 lemons
1 C ketchup

2 t Worcestershire
Black pepper and salt
Pinch of sugar
Dash of Mexi-pep

Mix at least 30 minutes before using and chill in refrigerator. Serve over shrimp or in a separate dish as a dip for boiled, fried, or barbecued shrimp.

VANNE'S CHEESE DIP

1 16-ounce package Velveeta cheese
1 can chilies and green peppers

Melt cheese and stir in chilies and green peppers (with some of the liquid drained off). Serve hot or cold.

VEGETABLE DIP

2/3 C mayonnaise	1 t Lawry's Seasoned
2/3 C sour cream	Salt
1 T dried onions	1 t Accent
1 T dried parsley	1 t dill seed

Mix all above and serve with fresh vegetables.

VEGETABLE DIP

1½ C sour cream	2 t salt
2½ C mayonnaise	½ t pepper
1 C finely chopped onion	¼ t Tabasco
1 C finely chopped	¼ t garlic powder
green pepper	(optional)
½ C finely chopped	
pimento	

Combine all ingredients in a large bowl and stir to blend well. Cover bowl and chill at least one hour or overnight. Makes 5 cups of dip.

NOTES

CHAMPAGNE PUNCH

1 6-oz. can frozen lemonade concentrate thawed
1 6-oz. can frozen pineapple juice thawed
6 6-oz. cans water
2 4/5 qt. bottles Riesling wine chilled
1 4/5 qt. bottle chamgagne chilled
1 20-oz. package whole frozen strawberries slightly
    thawed.

Pour lemonade and pineapple juice concentrate and water into punch bowl. Chill. Add wine and champagne just before serving. Float strawberries on punch. 18 ½ C. servings.

COFFEE ROYAL

2 qt. chilled coffee   2 qt. vanilla ice cream
1 C dark rum   1 C heavy cream, whipped
¾ C sugar

Combine all ingredients in a punch bowl in order listed and stir until ice cream is almost melted. Serve immediately. 30 punch cups.

COLD DUCK PUNCH

2 tall cans chilled red Hawaiian Punch
1 bottle cold Duck

Mix together and serve chilled.

DEEP FREEZE DAIQUIRI

2 6-oz. cans frozen pink lemonade
1 6 oz. can frozen limeade
1 fifth of light rum
6 lemonade cans of water

Mix together all ingredients. Store in glass jar in deep freeze 8-12 hours before serving. About 30 min. before serving, remove from freezer. Mixture should be icy. Any portion not used may be frozen again. You may want to omit 1 can pink lemonade and add 1-10 oz. package of frozen strawberries. For a tart taste add juice of 2 lemons. This mixture will never freeze solid, it will be a slush stage. This makes 2 qt. 20-25 cocktails.

HOT BUTTERED CRANBERRY PUNCH

¾ C brown sugar   **½ t. cinnamon**
1 C water   **½ t. ground allspice**
¼ t. salt   **¾ t. cloves**
¼ t. nutmeg

Make a syrup of above ingredients and boil for 5 min.

2 cans cranberry   **1 qt. pineapple juice**
3 C water   **¼ lb. butter**

Dissolve cranberry in water. Add juice and butter. To this mixture add syrup. Punch may be refrigerated. When ready to serve heat punch.

HOT LIQUID TEA

6 tea bags   6 C water

Steep tea bags in water for 5 minutes.

Add:
1 C sugar   ½ C pineapple juice
2 sticks cinnamon   ¼ C lemon juice
½ C orange juice

Boil 5 minutes.

KOOL ADE PUNCH

4 pkgs. lemon-lime Kool-ade   6 qts. water
2 large cans pineapple juice   4 C sugar
2 large bottles ginger ale

Serves 50 people. A delightful, inexpensive punch. Simple to make for large crowds.

ORANGE JUICE PUNCH

2 small cans frozen   1 qt. ginger ale
  orange juice   1 46-oz. can pineapple juice
1 small can frozen lemonade

Mix orange juice and lemonade as directed on can. Add pineapple juice. When ready to serve add ginger ale. May add ½ C or more sugar to make it sweeter if desired.

drinks

PEACH DAIQUIRIS

1 can lemonade mix   3 peaches, skinned and pitted
2 cans rum

Put above ingredients in blender. Fill blender to top with cracked ice and blend smooth.

PEACH FUZZ

1 small can pink lemonade
1 small can of gin (use lemonade can)
2 pkgs. frozen peaches unthawed

Put all the above ingredients into blender, finish filling blender to top with crushed ice. Blend and serve immediately.

PUNCH

1 doz. oranges, squeezed   1 doz. lemons, squeezed
1 pt. strong tea   1 C pineapple juice
1 pt. grape juice   sugar to taste
3 bottles rum

2 parts of this to 1 part ginger ale.

RUM DUMS

1 fifth light rum
2 small cans lemonade
   concentrate

4 lemonade cans water
2 12-oz. bottles ginger
   ale

Mix and pour in plastic container and put in freezer. Stir and serve.

RUM PUNCH

2 qt. rum
1 6-oz. can frozen limeade, thawed and undiluted
1 12-oz. bottle grenadine syrup
2 qt. carbonated water

Combine all ingredients except carbonated water in punch bowl.
Chill. Just before serving, add carbonated water and ice. 40 servings.

SANGRIA

1 banana, sliced
½ lemon, sliced
½ orange, sliced
½ apple, cut in thin wedges

¼ C superfine sugar
1 bottle dry red wine
¼ C brandy
club soda

Combine first seven ingredients and chill. Just before serving add
chilled club soda to taste. Delicious!

drinks

SPARKLING RECEPTION PUNCH

1 6-oz. can frozen lemonade concentrate
6 C (1 large can) pineapple juice
2 bottles white table wine
1 large bottle champagne or sparkling water

Combine frozen lemonade and pineapple juice in a punch bowl. Add white table wine and champagne. Mix well. Add large chunk of ice or ice ring. Serves approximately 100 small glasses.

SPICED TEA

2 C tang
½ C instant tea
1½ C sugar

1 pkg. lemon powder (Twist Imitation lemon)
1 T cinnamon
½ T powdered cloves

Mix well and store in tight container. Use 3 t per cup with hot water.

SWEETENED ICED TEA

4 qts. water
4 C sugar

4 lemons
1 C tea leaves

Place sugar in large enamel pot. Squeeze juice from lemons. Add juice, cut rind and tea. Pour boiling water over. Stir, let stand cool. Strain.

TOMATO REFRESHER

1 No. 2 can (2½ C) tomato juice
3 T lemon juice
1 t sugar

¼ t celery salt
1 t Worcestershire sauce

Combine ingredients, chill. Stir before serving. Float paper thin lemon slices a top. Makes five 4 oz. servings.

TUMBLE WEED (for 1)

1 oz. creme de Cacao
½ oz. coffee liqueur (Kahlua)
1 oz. milk

large scoop vanilla ice cream

Mix together in blender and serve.

TWENTY-FOUR HOUR COCKTAIL

8 oz. whiskey
8 oz. grapefruit juice
½ C sugar

½ C water
juice of 3 lemons
grated rind of 3 lemons

Squeeze lemons and blend rest of ingredients together. Let stand in refrigerator 24 hours. Strain and serve over cracked ice. Serves 12.

WASSAIL

1 C sugar	2 C orange juice
4 cinnamon sticks	6 C claret
lemon slices	½ C lemon juice
2 C pineapple juice	1 C dry sherry

Boil sugar, cinnamon sticks, and 3 lemon slices in ½ cup water for 5 minutes and strain. Heat but do not boil the remaining ingredients. Combine with syrup, garnish with lemon slices, and serve hot. Serves 20.

WEDDING PUNCH

2 oz. citric acid	1 qt. boiling water
6 oranges	1 qt. cold water
6 C sugar (tea cups)	

Squeeze oranges, grind orange rind and pulp. Add acid, sugar, and boiling water. Add to cold water, Drain-dilute 1 or 2 times as preferred to taste. Just before serving add 1 No. 2 can pineapple juice and 1 qt. ginger ale. Serves 35-40 cups.

WHISKEY SOUR PUNCH

1 6-oz. can frozen orange juice
1 qt. sparkling water or ginger ale
1 6-oz. can frozen lemonade.
½ C maraschino cherry juice
1 fifth bourbon

Mix orange juice and lemonade with water according to directions on cans. Pour them, cherry juice, sparkling water and bourbon over a block of ice in a punch bowl. Garnish with cherries and orange juice. Serves 15-20.

HOT APPLE CIDER PUNCH

1 gallon apple cider
2 t cloves
2 t whole allspice

2 3-inch cinnamon sticks
2/3 C sugar
2 oranges,
studded with cloves

Heat cider, cloves, allspice, cinnamon and sugar to boiling; cover and simmer 20 minutes. Strain punch and pour into punch bowl. Float oranges in bowl. Serves 32.

PARTY FRUIT PUNCH

1 40-oz. bottle grape juice
1 12-oz. can frozen
   orange juice
1 12-oz. can water
12-18 oranges, squeezed

1 small can pineapple juice
juice from small bottle
   maraschino cherries
2 C sugar
6 lemons, squeezed

Mix juices, water and sugar; let set 4 to 6 hours before serving. Pour into punch bowl over ice cubes. Add very thinly sliced lemon and orange. Makes approximately one gallon.

SHERBET PUNCH

2 32-oz. cans frozen
   orange juice
4 18-oz. cans frozen
   lemonade

4 6-oz. cans frozen
   pineapple juice
1 gallon pineapple
   sherbet

Add water to juice concentrates according to directions on cans. Chill and pour over sherbet just before serving. Recipe may be cut in half. Serves 50.

index

dips

drinks

METRIC SYSTEM

1 teaspoon		5 cubic centimeters
1 tablespoon	3 teaspoons	15 cubic centimeters
¼ cup	4 tablespoons	59.1 cubic centimeters
1 cup		236.5 cubic centimeters
1 pint	2 cups	473 cubic centimeters
1 quart	2 pints	946 cubic centimeters
1 gallon	4 quarts	3.785 liters
1 pound	16 ounces	454 grams

250 degrees Fahrenheit = 106 Centigrade
350 degrees Fahrenheit = 162 Centigrade
450 degrees Fahrenheit = 218 Centigrade

NOTES